BIBLE STUDY OUTLINES AND MESSAGES

Jim Burns and Mike DeVries

GENERAL
EDITOR

COMPILER

D1550861

Gospel Light

CL

Gospel Light is a Christian publisher dedicated to serving the local church. We believe God's vision for Gospel Light is to provide church leaders with biblical, user-friendly materials that will help them evangelize, disciple and minister to children, youth and families.

We hope this Gospel Light resource will help you discover biblical truth for your own life and help you minister to youth. God bless you in your work.

For a free catalog of resources from Gospel Light please contact your Christian supplier or call 1-800-4-GOSPEL or www.gospellight.com.

PUBLISHING STAFF
William T. Greig, Publisher
Dr. Elmer L. Towns, Senior Consulting Publisher
Dr. Gary S. Greig, Senior Consulting Editor
Jill Honodel, Editor
Pam Weston, Assistant Editor
Kyle Duncan, Associate Publisher
Bayard Taylor, M.Div., Editor, Theological and Biblical Issues
Debi Thayer, Designer

ISBN 0-8307-1885-0
© 1998 by Jim Burns
All rights reserved.
Printed in U.S.A.

HOW TO MAKE CLEAN COPIES FROM THIS BOOK

Contents

Bible Study Outlines

Scripture Reference Index

Special Thanks...

To all the high school students at Yorba Linda Friends Church: Being your pastor is one of life's incredible joys!

To Jon Irving, Kim Klein, Jill Willis, John Prevost, Kimberly Chamberlain and Megan Jones: You are the most incredible ministry team to work with. I love you guys!

Dedication

To my daughter Megan:
During the writing of this book you came into our lives. Mommy and I love you so very much, and so does Joshua! I'm so proud to be your daddy. I pray that I will always be exactly the dad you need me to be. I love you!

Mike DeVries
Yorba Linda Friends Church
Yorba Linda, California
NIYM

Contributors

MIKE DEVRIES
Flossing Away Anger and Bitterness
Attitude Check
Moses: Ordinary People Doing
       Extraordinary Things
Sticks and Stones: Taming the Tongue
Abraham: Laying It All on the Line
The Radical Forgiveness of God
God's Love Letter to You
Mine, Mine, All Mine: The Art of Giving
Knowing You're Not Alone
Falling in Love with Jesus
Seen and Not Heard
I've Changed My Mind!
What Happened to You?
Who Do You Listen To?
The Apple of His Eye
Me, Myself and I
Improving Your Serve
Handling the Heat: This Pressure Is Killing
      Me!
Being a Ficus for God
Surviving the Storm: The First Water Skier
Handling the Big *T*
No Thanks, I'd Rather Be Ungrateful!
All Stressed Out and No Place to Go!

Becoming a Great Christian
No Fear!
Just Do It!
Where Is God When It Hurts?
You're Not Like Me!
Getting the Ingredients Right
So You Want to Be a Wise Guy!

KARA ECKMANN
A Heartbreaker

STEVE ERNST
Now You See Him; Now You Don't
Happily Ever After

JIM LIEBELT
Forgive? Forget It!

MARK SIMONE
With Help from Little Friends
What a Character You Are!
What's Your Problem?

RUSS VAN NEST
Hey, You Got a Call from God!

Introduction

Someone once said, "The essence of creativity is the ability to copy." That is a very freeing statement for me personally. Of course, there is a major difference between plagiarizing someone's work and simply copying it. This outstanding book gives you a ton of great Bible study topics and message ideas to use with your group. What I like most about these ideas is that they have already been tried and they work with students.

One of our primary jobs as youth workers is to plant the Word of God into our students' lives so that it will take root and sprout spiritual growth. On the pages of this book are brilliant ways to communicate the Word of God to students. This book was put together by one of my favorite youth workers on Planet Earth— Mike DeVries. Most of the messages and Bible studies were written by him and he compiled others from key youth ministry leaders from around the country. Not only

does Mike lead one of the finest high school youth ministry departments in the world, but he has the ability to create material that is easily adaptable for others to use.

You may be wondering what the differences are between Message Outlines and Bible Study Outlines. The Message Outlines are written with predominantly large audiences in mind, providing a lecture format to be used in teaching a large group. The Bible Study Outlines are written to be used in a small group setting with more questions throughout the lesson, and therefore provide more interaction than the Message Outlines.

I think you will treasure the fourth volume of this *Fresh Ideas* series and return to it on a regular basis for refreshing new ideas on how to make the Bible come alive to the students of this generation.

There may not be a more important task in the Church than what you do in feeding

the Word of God to young people. May God bless your outstanding work with young people and may you catch just a small glimpse of the eternal difference you are making in the lives of those students in your youth ministry. God bless you.

Yours in Christ,
Jim Burns, Ph.D.
President,
National Institute of Youth Ministry
San Clemente, California

Message Outlines

Overview

Flossing Away Anger and Bitterness

TOPIC
Dealing with anger and bitterness

DESCRIPTION
Anger and bitterness are emotions that we all deal with, yet if we do not deal with them properly, they become destructive forces in our lives. This message teaches us how to "floss" away anger and bitterness.

KEY VERSE
"Get rid of all bitterness, rage and anger, brawling and slander, along with every form of malice. Be kind and compassionate to one another, forgiving each other, just as in Christ God forgave you." Ephesians 4:31,32

BIBLICAL BASIS
Proverbs 12:16; 15:1; 29:11; Ephesians 4:26,27,31,32; James 1:19

THE BIG IDEA
Anger and bitterness are emotions that will consume and ultimately destroy your life if not properly dealt with.

PREPARATION
- A roll of dental floss
- Poster board, cut into 15 pieces of approximately equal sizes
- Felt-tip pen

Using the 15 pieces of poster board, prepare five sets of signs with each set consisting of three signs with one of the following phrases printed on each one: "short fuse," "slow burn" and "no sweat."

Outline

Flossing Away Anger and Bitterness

INTRODUCTION

For the introduction you'll need the roll of dental floss and the five sets of signs you have previously prepared.

Invite five students up front. Ask the participants to hold up the sign that best fits their responses to each of the following situations as you read them. Be sure to allow time for each one to respond.

Anger–O–Meter

1. Someone tells you you're ugly.
2. Someone tells you you're worthless.
3. Someone insults your mother.
4. Someone cuts you off while you're driving.
5. Someone beats up your younger brother/sister.
6. Your brother/sister does something, then blames you, and your parents believe him/her!
7. A friend breaks a promise.
8. A friend talks about you behind your back.
9. Your boyfriend/girlfriend dumps you.
10. Your date is 45 minutes late picking you up.
11. Your friends seem to be ignoring you.
12. Someone you trusted with seriously personal information spreads it around.

Make the following observations:

- We get angry about a lot of things.
- Ephesians 4:26,27 says: "Don't give the devil a foothold."
- Not dealing with anger will give the devil a foothold in our lives.
- If we don't deal with the anger, it turns into bitterness.

Flossing Away Anger and Bitterness

Pull out the roll of dental floss, show it to the group and say something like the following:

> When we eat, food gets trapped between our teeth. Sometimes that food cannot be brushed out. If that food is left there, it produces bacteria that releases a destructive acid. If we don't remove the bacteria-producing particles by flossing regularly, our gums will rot and stop supplying nourishment to our teeth and our teeth will eventually fall out!
>
> Anger and bitterness are just like that. Every day we encounter people, problems and issues that seem to stick in our mind. If left alone they will turn into bacteria that will release the acid of bitterness into our lives and ultimately destroy our joy.

The Big Idea: Anger and bitterness are emotions that will consume and ultimately destroy your life if not properly dealt with.

BODY OF THE MESSAGE

"Get rid of all bitterness, rage and anger, brawling and slander, along with every form of malice. Be kind and compassionate to one another, forgiving each other, just as in Christ God forgave you." Ephesians 4:31,32

I. Admit the Anger

   A. When you're angry, admit it.
   B. Anger is normal—the problem is what you do with it.
   C. Choose to deal with it.
   D. Choose to not let it stagnate or fester.

II. Get a Grip

   A. Proverbs 29:11: "A fool gives full vent to his anger, but a wise man keeps himself under control."
   B. When you are angry, ask yourself the Big Three:
     1. What am I angry about?
     2. Why am I so angry?
     3. What do I need to do about it? (i.e., What would Jesus do?)

III. Keep Short Accounts

A. Ephesians 4:26 (*NLT*): "Don't sin....Don't let the sun go down while you are still angry."
B. We need to keep short accounts. When something happens, deal with it as soon as possible:
  1. Go to the person you are angry with.
  2. Speak with gentleness (see Proverbs 15:1).
  3. Go to talk and listen, not to blow up (see James 1:19).
C. Issues may seem insignificant, but so does that small leftover piece of Big Mac between your teeth until it becomes decayed.

IV. Forgive

A. Read Ephesians 4:31,32: Forgiveness is the key!
B. We need to forgive completely, regardless of the other person's actions or response.
C. Lack of forgiveness only leads to bitterness; it consumes and destroys.

V. Let It Go

A. Part of forgiveness is letting go of the need for revenge or to punish the one who hurt you. If not, we don't fully forgive.
B. Letting it go means letting the person who hurt you off the hook (see Proverbs 12:16)!

CHALLENGE/ACTION STEPS

- Don't let anger fester; it only produces bitterness.
- Review the main points.
- Hand out a piece of dental floss to everyone in the group as a reminder of what you talked about. Have them tie it to something that will remind them of what you talked about.

Flossing Away Anger and Bitterness

1. When was the last time you got really angry? What happened? Did it get resolved?

2. What are some ways people react when they get angry over a situation?

3. What do you think Ephesians 4:26 means?

4. How do you deal with anger? Is it hard? Why or why not?

   How do you tend to deal with it when someone is angry with you?

5. How do anger and bitterness destroy someone?

6. What is something you heard today that makes sense in dealing with anger?

   What will you do with this new information?

Overview

Attitude Check

TOPIC
Examining your attitude

DESCRIPTION
This study explores what kinds of attitudes we have now and what it takes to change our attitudes to be more Christlike.

KEY VERSE
"Your attitude should be the same as that of Christ Jesus." Philippians 2:5

BIBLICAL BASIS
Job 42:5; John 8:1-11; Philippians 2:3-5; 4:6,7; 1 Thessalonians 5:18

THE BIG IDEA
Your circumstances may never change, but your attitude can—and that makes all the difference in the world.

PREPARATION
For Introduction:
- A jar with a lid
- Saltshaker filled with salt
- Sand
- Ordinary dirt
- A container of water

Have all the ingredients set up on a table before the meeting begins.

Outline

Attitude Check

INTRODUCTION

Surviving the Shaker

Explain:

We all go through tough times in our lives. Our lives are a lot like this jar. *(Fill the jar with water.)* As we go through life, things happen; tough times come. *(Add salt, sand and dirt to the water in the jar. Put the lid on the jar.)* Tough circumstances come along and shake up our lives *(Shake the jar)* and cloud our vision.

Discuss the following issues:
- The condition of the mixture before and after shaking—before: clear, easy; after: murky, clouded
- Circumstances are like the shaker, revealing what your life is made of.
- When you go through tough times, the real you is seen.
- What comes out is your true attitude towards self, others and God.

> **The Big Idea:** Your circumstances may never change, but your attitude can—and that makes all the difference in the world!

If you can change your circumstances—great! If not, you'll need to change your attitude.

Challenge your students to take an attitude check and see if it needs a change!

BODY OF THE MESSAGE: ATTITUDE CHECK

I. Examine Your Attitude

A. Are you critical or thankful?
1. It's easy to be critical of others and complain about situations.
2. Criticism and negativity will come back to haunt you and you end up being critical of yourself.

3. God calls us to be thankful (see 1 Thessalonians 5:18).

4. Be thankful in all situations—even the ones that you don't like being in!

B. Are you selfish or selfless?

1. Are you always looking at situations for "What's in it for me?" or "What can I get?"

2. Scripture calls us to look out for the interests of others (see Philippians 2:3,4).

3. Are you looking out for Number One, or are you looking out for those around you?

4. If you're only looking out for yourself, what happens when you're in need?

C. Are you apathetic or passionate?

1. One of the biggest hurdles to overcome is apathy—a lack of passion.

2. In your circumstances, is your attitude one of "I just don't care"?

3. I believe that what God is looking for are people who care and are passionate about the world around them.

D. Are you prideful or humble?

1. When things are going your way, what's your attitude like?

2. Do you think that things are going great because of your own strength, talent or luck?

3. God is the One who is in control and He's the One who is at work.

4. God is looking for people who are humble and who recognize that He is in control.

> **The Big Idea:** Your circumstances may never change, but your attitude can—and that makes all the difference in the world.

II. Change Your Attitude

A. See others as God sees them

1. How do you see others? As God does?

2. Read John 8:1-11, an example of seeing others through the eyes of Jesus.

3. Jesus saw into the heart of the woman caught in adultery and He knew her potential. He didn't condone what she did, but He didn't condemn her either.

4. Do you see others as Jesus sees them?

5. How you see those around you will affect your attitude and ultimately how you treat them!

B. See situations as God sees them

1. When tough times come, how do you respond?

2. When your jar gets shaken, what comes to the surface in your life?

3. Do you see your circumstances as a God-given opportunity for growth?

4. Read Job 42:5—Job heard about God before his trials, but at the end of his trials, he *saw* God.

C. See yourself as God sees you

1. So many times we are paralyzed by what we see in the mirror of our lives.

2. Tough times come and we become paralyzed with self-doubt and fear.

3. God sees such incredible potential in each one of us.

4. We are an unrepeatable miracle, loved for who we are—not what we do!

D. See the future as God sees it

1. God sees the future for what it can be—He sees past the tough times.

2. Are you apathetic? Do you not see any hope?

3. God sees the possibilities of your future.

4 Your attitude is your choice. Will it be one that says, *There's nothing I can do* or *Things can be different and will be*!

CHALLENGE/ACTION STEPS

• What comes to the surface when your life is shaken like this jar?

• Your Christlike attitude toward people and circumstances is essential in surviving tough times.

Review

• Examine your attitude. Does it need to be changed?

• Change your attitude where it needs to be changed.

• Spend some time in guided prayer, praying through each aspect of "Examine Your Attitude" and "Change Your Attitude."

• Give students time to talk with God about their attitudes and what they need to do to improve.

After the following discussion time, invite students to pray together in their small groups for the circumstances that are brought up during the discussion and are in need of being turned over to God. Also pray for those who share that God would give each of them the strength to live above their circumstances.

Attitude Check

1. Which of the four attitude checks can you identify with?

Critical _____ or _____ Thankful
1   5   10

Selfish _____ or _____ Selfless
1   5   10

Apathetic _____ or _____ Passionate
1   5   10

Prideful _____ or _____ Humble
1   5   10

2. What makes it tough to apply this message?

3. What concepts are found in Philippians 4:6,7 that will guarantee us peace in the midst of tough times?

4. In what areas/situations of your life do you most need an attitude check?

5. What circumstance in your life do you need to turn over to God?

6. What steps can you take in your own life to live beyond your circumstances?

Overview

Moses: Ordinary People Doing Extraordinary Things

TOPIC
Ordinary people being used in extraordinary ways by an extraordinary God

DESCRIPTION
God is in the business of recycling broken lives. There is perhaps no greater news for our students this day than that God desires to use them, regardless of their pasts, their excuses and their obstacles. This message takes a look at the life of Moses—a man who definitely was ordinary and had a flawed past—yet God saw something in Moses that Moses didn't see. He chose to use Moses to lead His people out of Egypt. Your students need to know that God wants to use them, flaws and all, to make an impact for the kingdom of God.

KEY VERSE
"I can do everything through him who gives me strength." Philippians 4:13

BIBLICAL BASIS
Exodus 2:11-15; 3:1-11; 4:1-13; 14:10-16,21-28; Philippians 4:13

THE BIG IDEA
God wants to use us to do some incredible things for His kingdom. We only need to be available and obedient.

PREPARATION
- A copy of *The Tale of Three Trees* by Angela Elwell Hunt (Colorado Springs, Colo.: Lion Publishing, A Division of Chariot Family Publishing, 1989)

Read through the book a few times to familiarize yourself with the story.

Outline

Moses: Ordinary People Doing Extraordinary Things

INTRODUCTION

The Tale of Three Trees[1]

Read the story to your group as a way to introduce the message, then make the following observations:

- We may think that God wants to use us in big ways for the kingdom of God—to change the world single-handedly—but in actuality God is looking for people to be available and obedient to Him.
- God isn't looking for the biggest, the best, the brightest. He's looking for ordinary people, like you and me, who will place themselves in His hands to be used.
- Recycling:
  - Turning something that seems useless into something that is useful.
  - God is in the business of recycling hearts and lives!
- God chooses things that seem useless and broken and turns them into something useful. God chooses ordinary people to accomplish His extraordinary work.

Today, we're going to look at one of the most seemingly useless people who God used to do big things—Moses!

> **The Big Idea:** God wants to use us to do some incredible things for His kingdom. We only need to be available and obedient.

You may be thinking *You've got to be kidding. Me do something big for God? No way!* But God does want to use you!

BODY OF THE MESSAGE: BEING USED BY GOD

I. God Is Bigger Than Your Past

A. Moses was a guy who had quite a past (see Exodus 2:11-15).

B. God knew all about Moses' past.

C. God saw something in Moses that Moses didn't even see in himself. In spite of everything God still chose to use him.

D. God sees your past. He sees something inside of you that you may not even see.

E. In spite of your weaknesses and failures, He still chooses you—He wants to use you!

II. God Is Bigger Than Your Excuses

A. God calls Moses (see Exodus 3:1-10).

B. Moses, instead of jumping for joy at being called to serve God, voices questions and doubts and offers excuses (see vv. 3:11-13; 4:1-13)!

  1. "Who am I, that I should go to Pharaoh and bring the Israelites out of Egypt?" (v. 3:11)

  2. I don't know what to do...what should I do? (v. 3:13).

  3. What if they laugh at me and don't believe me? (v. 4:1).

  4. I don't have what it takes; I'm not talented enough! (v. 4:10).

  5. Don't you have anyone else who can do it? (v. 4:13).

C. Moses was fearful and doubtful of his own abilities—just like us!

D. All the time, God just told Moses to focus on who He was and what He could do!

E. Even through all Moses' excuses, it didn't change how God felt about him or disqualify him from what God wanted to do!

F. We're just like Moses!

III. God Is Bigger Than Your Obstacles

A. Moses returned to Egypt, not knowing what obstacles would be in his way (i.e., Pharaoh's hardened heart, Egyptian soldiers, even the Israelites).

B. God was faithful to Moses. He removed all the obstacles and worked through Moses to bring the Israelites out of Egypt.

C. The Red Sea was a pretty *big* obstacle—1,200 miles long, 130 to 230 miles wide and at the deepest part 7,200 feet deep! Not a small puddle!

D. God, don't fail me now (see Exodus 14:10-16)!

E. God pulls through (see Exodus 14:21-28).

F. There will be many obstacles in our lives (give examples from your own life).

G. God is bigger than any obstacle you have in your way. He is willing to part the sea to use you!

CHALLENGE/ACTION STEPS

- God is in the business of using ordinary people to accomplish extraordinary things for His kingdom.
- He wants to use you.

REVIEW

- God is bigger than... (list various difficulties or problems your students might be facing right now).
- Want to be used by God?
  1. **Be available:** Are you making yourself available to Him?
     - Don't wait for your problems to get solved or your obstacles to get removed.
     - Don't spend your life preparing and planning to be used—someday.
     - Make yourself available to Him today!
  2. **Be action oriented:** Do something about it!
     - Be ready for action.

Note:
1.   For more storybook ideas, check out *Fresh Ideas Resource 2: Case Studies, Talk Sheets & Discussion Starters* by Jim Burns and Mark Simone (Ventura, Calif.: Gospel Light, 1997), pp. 97-102.

Moses: Ordinary People Doing Extraordinary Things

1. Moses didn't have the perfect past. In fact, Moses wasn't perfect at all! Why do you think God chose to use him for such a great task?

2. Do you ever wonder if God has anything great He would like you to do? If so, what?

3. If God chose to use you to do something great for His kingdom, what would you say?

4. What are some of the excuses that you give God when faced with being used for something great, or with something small?

5. What gifts, talents and abilities do you think you have to offer God?

6. What can you do this week to use your talents, gifts and/or abilities for the kingdom of God?

7. If you could do something great for the kingdom of God, knowing you'd never fail, what would you want to do?

Overview

Sticks and Stones: Taming the Tongue

TOPIC
The power of our words on other people's lives

DESCRIPTION
Each one of us possesses the most powerful weapon in the world—words. "Sticks and stones may break my bones but words will never hurt me!" is the old saying. Yet in our world, we know the truth—words do hurt us. Scripture calls us to weigh our words carefully, knowing that within them lies the power to build others up or to destroy those around us. This message examines the power of our words and how we can use them to build up or tear down others.

KEY VERSE
"Do not let any unwholesome talk come out of your mouths, but only what is helpful for building others up according to their needs, that it may benefit those who listen." Ephesians 4:29

BIBLICAL BASIS
Matthew 12:34-37; Acts 9:26,27; 11:22,23; 15:37-40; Ephesians 4:29; 5:4; Hebrews 10:24,25; James 3:1-12

THE BIG IDEA
The words you speak have the power to build up or tear down those around you.

PREPARATION
For Introduction:
- Trash can (with lots of trash, the dirtier the better)
- Mirror
- Gift-wrapped box

Prepare and gather the materials and set them on a table.

For Challenge/Action Steps:
- Note cards and envelopes
- Pens or pencils

For Discussion Starters:
- Ball of yarn

Outline

Sticks and Stones: Taming the Tongue

INTRODUCTION

Are the Words We Speak Constructive or Destructive?

Hold up the trash can, then the mirror and finally the gift-wrapped box. As you hold up each item in turn, ask the group:

How does this item represent the words that we speak?

Allow students time to respond before going on to the next item. When they make their responses, ask them to clarify and give examples or Scripture verses that explain their insight.

Either after each item is discussed or after all three have been held up and discussed, be sure to explain the following insights:

- **The trash can**—Sometimes our words are filthy just like this filthy trash can; no one wants to be around us. Sometimes the words that we speak are as useless as stinking garbage in building others up (see Ephesians 4:29; 5:4).
- **The mirror**—Our words reflect what's in our hearts—whether good or bad (see Matthew 12:34-37). Our words can reflect what God thinks about a person. Our words can show someone what is inside of them, even if they don't see it. Our words reflect the depth of our relationships with God.
- **The gift**—Our words can be a gift of encouragement in the lives of others. Just as people treasure certain gifts, our words can be treasures in people's hearts—things they will hold on to when they are discouraged or lonely. Our words can bring a smile to someone's day. Our words of encouragement are a gift of God to others (see Hebrews 10:24,25).[2]

Our words are powerful! They can either be:
1. Destructive—for example:
   - Gossip, put-downs, "sticks and stones"

- We believe what we hear and we become what we believe ourselves to be.
2. Constructive: Ephesians 4:29
   - What kind of words do you use? Are they constructive or destructive?

Let's check out someone who knew how to tame the tongue—Barnabas, the son of encouragement.

BODY OF THE MESSAGE—BARNABAS: TAMING THE TONGUE

I. Believe in Others (Acts 9:26,27)

A. Look for the potential in others. Barnabas saw the potential in Paul, even when the disciples didn't.
B. When everyone else saw the outside, Barnabas saw the inside.
C. Regard others not as they are, but as who they could become.
D. There's power in someone who can see beyond the outside, seeing what God sees in others!
E. Are you that type of person?

II. Build Others Up (Acts 11:22,23)

A. Let others know what you see in them.
B. More than just seeing their potential, we need to take the opportunity to tell them!
C. Challenge them to live up to that potential.
D. Encourage them to be all that God sees in them (see Hebrews 10:24,25). Let us consider...
   - Spurring one another on;
   - Toward love and good deeds;
   - Meeting together;
   - Encouraging each other.

III. Be Active with Encouragement (Acts 15:37-40)

A. Barnabas and John Mark: from a failure to a fellow worker, Barnabas saw the potential in John Mark despite his failure. He let him know it, and took the opportunity to encourage him.
B. Do something about what you see in others and tell them.
C. Be active in encouraging others.
D. Be liberal, but honest, with praise.
E. Be vocal with your encouragement.

F. Look for ways to express your belief in and/or encouragement of others:
    1. Face-to-face
    2. With a note
    3. Over the phone

CHALLENGE/ACTION STEPS

- There is power in our words!
- What are the words that you speak—constructive or destructive?
- Tame your tongue like Barnabas.
    1. Believe in others.
    2. Build others up.
    3. Be active with your encouragement.
- Your encouragement could change someone's life!
    1. Who in your life needs to be encouraged this week?
    2. What and when will you do something about it?

Letters of Encouragement

Give each student a note card, envelope and pen or pencil. Have them write notes of encouragement to someone they know who needs it. Either have them deliver their notes or send them through the mail.

Affirmation Yarn

Begin the discussion time with the following activity to give students an opportunity to experience the power of words firsthand.

With the ball of yarn in hand, tell students that they will be practicing what they have just heard. Unwrap the ball of yarn, and while holding onto the end of the yarn in one hand and the ball of yarn in the other hand, select a person and say something encouraging to him or her. After you are finished, throw that person the ball of yarn. Now that person needs to select a person to encourage, then throw the ball to that person. Continue until everyone has been encouraged and you have finished your ball of yarn.

Ask everyone to continue holding onto the yarn for the rest of your time together as a group while you discuss the questions on the next page. (Be sure to bring out the fact that as your group is bound together by the common string you are holding, so encouragement binds them together as a group.)

Note:
2. For more object lessons, check out *Fresh Ideas Resource 2: Case Studies, Talk Sheets & Discussion Starters* by Jim Burns and Mark Simone (Ventura, Calif.: Gospel Light, 1997), pp. 55-69.

Sticks and Stones: Taming the Tongue

1. How did it feel to be encouraged?

2. What surprised you about the encouragement you received?

3. What is it that holds us back from being more encouraging to others?

4. What are some benefits and blessings that come from being an encourager?

5. How does encouragement build others up and minister to them?

6. Who are three people that you know who need your encouragement?

7. What are some ways you can and will build them up?

8. What are some ways you can be active in your encouragement? What will you do this week to be more of an encourager?

Overview

A Heartbreaker

TOPIC
Having a heart for the lost

DESCRIPTION
Lost people matter to God, and they should matter to us as Christians. God's heart breaks for those people who do not know Him. His calling for each of us as Christians is that our hearts would be broken for the lost as well. This message examines God's heart for the lost and how we can reach out to those who are lost.

KEY VERSE
"Then he said to his disciples, 'The harvest is plentiful but the workers are few. Ask the Lord of the harvest, therefore, to send out workers into his harvest field.'" Matthew 9:37,38

BIBLICAL BASIS
Matthew 9:35-38; 2 Corinthians 5:17-20; 2 Peter 3:9

THE BIG IDEA
Sharing Jesus flows from being heartbroken over the lost and understanding our own emptiness without Jesus.

PREPARATION
- A two- to three-foot-long piece of 2x4 lumber
- A hammer
- Some nails

Have the items set up on a table.

Outline

A Heartbreaker

INTRODUCTION

Introduce the message by saying:

Close your eyes and picture your school campus in your mind: Band area, drama area, academic area, jock area, senior area. (Give them a few seconds to visualize.)

Now, imagine Jesus on your campus:
- What would He see?
- What would He feel?
- What would He do?

Jesus is already on your campus—through you.
You are an ambassador for Christ (see 2 Corinthians 5:17-20).
Your response should be like His as you are being transformed into His image.

BODY OF THE MESSAGE

Read Matthew 9:35-38.

I. How heartbroken are you for the lost?

Being heartbroken for the lost means:
- Losing sleep over their souls;
- Feeling burdened to pray for them;
- Developing deeper friendships to understand them.

Hammer and Nail Illustration

Refer to the piece of wood, hammer and nails. Pound the nails into the piece of wood as you explain people's emptiness without God.

The following are a few general areas of need that you could describe as you pound nails into the wood (one nail for each need):

- In elementary school: wore glasses, braces; was made fun of.
- In junior high: felt outside the popular group.
- In high school: did not receive grades wanted, not asked to dance by guy/girl you wanted, family arguments, didn't make it on the sports team you wanted, thought about suicide, eating disorder, abuse.
- All these things are like nails being pounded into the wood of your heart—leaving scars, hurts, pain and a feeling of lostness.

II. In feeling lost, people tend to do one of two things:

Denial: They live in superficiality, pretending to be strong.
Despair: They live in self-pity, acting helpless.

A. The gospel comes between these two reactions.
B. You, as a messenger of the gospel, can come between these two reactions.
C. You will never share Jesus until you believe your friends need to hear it.
D. You will never believe your friends need to hear the gospel unless you're heartbroken for them.
E. The way we minister to people who are lost and need Jesus is to understand how we ourselves are lost without Jesus.
F. We were just like them: same wood, same nail holes.

C.S. Lewis said, "Think of me as a fellow patient in the same hospital who, having been admitted a little earlier, could give some advice."

CHALLENGE/ACTION STEPS

Read the following story to students:

I've Seen Your Scars

There was a man who was in a car accident and went flying through the windshield. He skidded and bumped his way along the pavement and ended up in a crumpled mass yards from his car.

He was knocked unconscious and only regained consciousness as he was being taken

in the ambulance to the hospital. His head was strapped to a back board because his spinal cord had been fractured and the slightest move of his head could paralyze him for life. He went through multiple surgeries, all of which stabilized his spinal cord, but he still had to spend six months wearing a metal halo on his head. It was attached to his head through several screws that went into his forehead and enabled the halo to rest on his head.

At the end of six months, he was totally healed, but he still had scars from the screws that had kept the metal halo fixed to his skull. He had two little holes on his forehead, but he was so tired of surgeries and hospitals that he decided not to have plastic surgery and to stick with the scars.

After a while, he felt God calling him into ministry to people who were in hospitals. He would visit people at their bedsides, pray with them and share Scripture with them if they were open to it.

One day he was summoned to visit a hardened motorcycle rider who several people had tried to share the gospel with, but no one could get through to him. He sat down next to the mangled motorcyclist's bed and began to talk with him. The motorcycle rider pretty much ignored him for a few minutes, but just as he was ready to give up and leave the room, the motorcycle rider noticed the two scars on his head.

"Wait a minute," he said. "I see your scars. You've been through something."

And that was the open door that he needed to share his experiences. After several more visits, the motorcycle rider accepted Jesus. Why? Because of this man's scars—because of his willingness to be a wounded healer.

- The lie is that we have to be perfect to minister. No, we need to be broken: broken-hearted, wounded people who have found the great healer and long for others to find Him also.
- Ask God to break your heart.
- Ask God to work through your woundedness.
- Is there someone you know who needs to hear about the love of Jesus Christ? Reach out to him or her!

A Heartbreaker

1. Who do you see on your school campus at lunch?

2. How would Jesus view them?

3. What scars do you see on your friends?

4. What scars do you have yourself?

5. How could God use your scars to reach out to other scarred and hurting people?

6. What will you do about it this week?

7. How can we help each other reach out to those who are lost and hurting?

Overview

Abraham: Laying It All on the Line

TOPIC
Faith

DESCRIPTION
Being a Christian means living your life by faith, and in God's Word there is no better example of what faith is all about than Abraham in Genesis 22. In this message, we'll be looking at what made Abraham tick. He's known as a great man of faith, but what does faith look like? How can we have that same life-changing faith?

KEY VERSE
"'Do not lay a hand on the boy,' he said. 'Do not do anything to him. Now I know that you fear God, because you have not withheld from me your son, your only son.'" Genesis 22:12

BIBLICAL BASIS
Genesis 22:1-18; Romans 4:18-21; Hebrews 11:1,6,17,18

THE BIG IDEA
Walking with God means walking by faith.

PREPARATION
For Introduction Option One:
• Costumes for the "spontaneous melodrama"
For Introduction Option Two:
• *Indiana Jones and the Last Crusade* video (Paramount Studios, Lucasfilm, Ltd., 1989)
Prepare the video clip by finding the part where Indiana Jones is about to take his "step of faith" to cross the chasm to the chamber where the Holy Grail was kept.

Outline

Abraham: Laying It All on the Line

INTRODUCTION

Option One: Now That's Faith!

A Day in the Life of...

(A spontaneous melodrama adapted from Genesis 22:1-18)

Select nine people for the following roles:

Abraham	two people to be the altar
Isaac	the Angel of the Lord
two servants	one ram
one donkey	

Adding costumes will enhance the melodrama. Have the "actors" stand offstage until they are read into the scene. Be sure to encourage them to ham it up as much as possible for the effect.

Read Genesis 22:1-18. Be sure to pause at appropriate times for the actors to have time to act out their parts.

After the melodrama, discuss the following issues:

- Abraham's life was a life of complete faith in God.
- Abraham walked with God, but more importantly, he believed God!

The Big Idea: Walking with God means walking by faith.

Option Two: A Step of Faith

Introduce the video segment by saying:

Faith is more than just a belief; it requires action—stepping out. What you are about to see is an excellent example of what faith is all about. Faith is not just believing something, it's taking action on what you believe.

Begin the clip from the part where Indiana Jones is about to take his "step of faith" across the chasm to get to the chamber where the Holy Grail was kept and stop the clip when he successfully crosses the chasm to get to the chamber.[3]

After the video segment, discuss the following issues:

- Why it is tough to step out in faith;
- Things that keep us from acting on our faith.

BODY OF THE MESSAGE: HAVING A LIFE-CHANGING FAITH!

I. Faith Isn't Always Comfortable

A. Faith isn't easy; it's tough (walking/living by faith is tough).
B. We're faced with all kinds of situations where we need to respond with faith: a math test, asking someone out on a date, taking the test for a driver's license, finances, divorce.
C. It's tough to step out/live out faith.
D. For Abraham, God asked him to do some tough things (sacrifice his *only* son).
E. Faith isn't easy, or it wouldn't be called "faith"!

II. Faith Is Being Fully Convinced

A. Faith is doing the right thing, even though you may not know how it will all work out in the end.
B. Abraham was fully convinced. He knew that God was faithful to His promise of many descendants, even though Isaac would be dead. Abraham didn't know how God was going to work it out, but he was convinced that God would be able to.
C. Faith doesn't demand all the answers. If it did, it would be fact, not faith.
D. Faith is trusting God when nothing makes sense and the answers aren't apparent.

III. Faith Is Being Fully Committed

A. Faith is being committed to God with 100 percent of your life.
B. Abraham was fully committed to God. He put God first in his life.
C. Abraham trusted and loved God enough to give up Isaac, his only son.
D. God tested Abraham's faith by seeing if Abraham loved his son more than he loved God. Genesis 22:16— "'You have obeyed me and have not withheld even your beloved son'" (*NLT*).
E. Faith is putting God first in your life, ahead of all else.

IV. Faith Is a Continual Process

A. Faith is something we utilize every day (driving in a car, sitting in a seat, etc.).

B. Faith is a process of growth that God uses in our lives.

C. When our faith is tested, it becomes easier to step out the next time, because we've seen God to be faithful.

D. This was not the first time Abraham walked by faith. God asked him...

    1. To leave his country;

    2. To wander about to find a land he did not know;

    3. To sacrifice what seemed to be his only hope of God's promise.

E. Every time that Abraham was tested and had to lean on his faith, he got stronger.

F. When we are tested in a situation and respond in faith, we are made stronger. Next time, it'll be easier to respond in faith.

CHALLENGE/ACTION STEPS

1. Ask the following questions, allowing students time to think through each question and answer in private:

    a. Are you convinced that God knows how the plan goes together?

    Is there something in your life right now about which God is asking you to have faith?

    Are you willing to respond and act in faith, even though you don't know all the answers?

    b. Are you committed to putting God first/obeying Him in faith?

    Is there something in your life that is coming before your love for God?

    What would you put in the blank: For I know that God is first in your life—you have not withheld even _____ from me?

    Give that area over to God.

2. Review the Four Cs.
    1. Faith isn't always *comfortable.*
    2. Faith is being fully *convinced.*
    3. Faith is being fully *committed.*
    4. Faith is a *continual process.*

Note:
3. For more video clip ideas, check out *Fresh Ideas Resource 2: Case Studies, Talk Sheets & Discussion Starters* by Jim Burns and Mark Simone (Ventura, Calif.: Gospel Light, 1997), pp. 103-113.

Abraham: Laying It All on the Line

1. Why is it tough to live by faith?

2. When was a time that you lived by faith?

3. What do the following verses say about faith?

   Romans 4:18-21

   Hebrews 11:1

   Hebrews 11:6

   Hebrews 11:17,18

4. What does it mean to be fully convinced?

   How does that impact faith?

APPLICATION: BRINGING IT HOME

Being Fully Convinced

What situation in your life right now is God asking you to be "fully convinced" that He will pull you through?

Being Fully Committed

What area do you need to give over to God?

What would you put in the blank: For I know that God is first in your life because you have not withheld even _____ from me!

What is one thing that you heard and/or learned today that will change the way you live?

How will it change your life?

Overview

Mine, Mine, All Mine: The Art of Giving

TOPIC
Stewardship, giving and materialism

DESCRIPTION
We live in a materialistic world. We seem to judge people's worth and value by the possessions they have. Yet God has a different plan. Everything we have is a gift from Him. Therefore, He calls us to be good stewards of what He has given to us. This message challenges students to view all they have through the eyes of God.

KEY VERSE
"People who want to get rich fall into temptation and a trap and into many foolish and harmful desires that plunge men into ruin and destruction. For the love of money is a root of all kinds of evil. Some people, eager for money, have wandered from the faith and pierced themselves with many griefs." 1 Timothy 6:9,10

BIBLICAL BASIS
Genesis 22:1-16; Matthew 6:1-4; 2 Corinthians 9:6-8; 1 Timothy 6:9,10

THE BIG IDEA
Our giving is a reflection of our love and obedience for God.

PREPARATION
- *Ali Baba Bunny* video clip: "Mine, Mine, All Mine!" (*Warner Bros. Cartoons Golden Jubilee Bugs Bunny's Wacky Adventures;* Warner Bros. Inc., 1985)
- VCR and TV

Find the beginning of the part titled "Mine, Mine, All Mine!" Be prepared to show the whole cartoon.

Outline

Mine, Mine, All Mine: The Art of Giving

INTRODUCTION

Givers and Takers

Make the following points:

- We live in a world that is selfish—focused on Number One.
- Selfishness consumes and destroys us!

Read 1 Timothy 6:9,10.

"Mine, Mine, All Mine!"

This Warner Brothers cartoon starring Bugs Bunny and Daffy Duck is an excellent tool in challenging your students with materialism, greed and giving. Daffy Duck finds a hidden treasure and tries to hoard it all for himself. The results are hilarious and will keep your kids talking for weeks about the effects of materialism. The classic line from the cartoon is "Mine, mine, all mine!" Show the entire cartoon, which lasts only about five to eight minutes.[4]

> **The Big Idea:** Our giving is a reflection of our love and obedience for God.

We give...

- Out of love for God;
- As an expression of gratitude;
- In obedience to His command;
- By putting our faith into action.

BODY OF THE MESSAGE: THE ART OF GIVING

I. God Wants 100 Percent of Your Life, Relationships and Possessions

A. God wants all of your heart and life.

B. The Bible tells us that if we want to follow Jesus, we need to love Him more than anything or anyone else.

C. God doesn't want just a part of your life—He wants it all.

D. The story of Abraham/Isaac (see Genesis 22:1-16): What's your Isaac? What is the thing you love more than and/or put before God?

E. God wants 100 percent of our lives, not out of duty, but out of love and as a response to what He has done for us.

II. God Wants a Percentage of Your Time

A. God also wants a part of your time.

B. How much time do you give God—in worship, service and time with Him?

C. Do you spend time with the ones you love? If you love God, you'll want to spend time with Him.

D. What we give our time to is what we value in our lives.

E. Love is spelled t-i-m-e. Where you spend your time shows where your heart is.

F. What percent of your time do you give God?

III. God Wants a Percentage of Your Treasure

A. In the Old Testament, a tithe (10 percent) was required by the Law.

B. In the New Testament, we are not under the Law. We are called to give from the heart, to give from what we've been given.

C. Attitude is more important than the amount.

D. God calls us to be faithful with what He has given us.

E. No matter how much you give, God is more concerned about your attitude and heart in giving.

> **The Big Idea:** Our giving is a reflection of our love and obedience for God.

F. That's our challenge—to become incredible givers.

How do we perfect the art of giving?

IV. Attitude of Giving—Perfecting the Art: G-I-V-E

Read 2 Corinthians 9:6-8.

A. **G**enerously (see 2 Corinthians 9:6)

1. The amount is not necessarily the important thing, but giving sacrificially is.

2. The key in giving is to rely on God.

3. Give back to God a portion of what He's generously given you.

4. God *will* meet your needs (see 2 Corinthians 9:8).

B. Individually (see 2 Corinthians 9:7)
  1. Personally decide what to give—it's between you and God!
  2. Personally get involved in your giving:
- Pray about your giving—ask God to use what you give.
- Pray about the church/youth ministry.
- Give your time to where you give your treasure.
C. Voluntarily (see 2 Corinthians 9:7)
  1. Giving should be something that you want to do, not have to do!
  2. Give joyfully. God loves a cheerful giver!
  3. Giving is a response of love, not a response to arm-twisting!
D. Everything without credit (see Matthew 6:1-4)
  1. Give in secret.
  2. Do not bring attention to yourself.
  3. Truly unselfish givers are embarrassed when their name is brought into the spotlight with their giving.

> **The Big Idea:** Our giving is a reflection of our love and obedience for God.

CHALLENGE/ACTION STEPS

Review G–I–V–E

1. **G**enerously
2. **I**ndividually
3. **V**oluntarily
4. **E**verything without credit

Provide your students with an opportunity to give to something over the next few weeks, or even months. The project needs to be something visible—something that shows students the difference their giving has made.

Be creative: the project could be a child sponsorship, service project, mission project, collecting money for the homeless, collecting money to make improvements on the church facilities, sponsoring a field trip for inner-city school children, or collecting money to help someone in need in the church or youth ministry. Take some time to think through a project that would get your students involved.

Note:
4. For more video clip ideas, check out *Fresh Ideas Resource 2: Case Studies, Talk Sheets & Discussion Starters* by Jim Burns and Mark Simone (Ventura, Calif.: Gospel Light, 1997), pp. 103-114.

Mine, Mine, All Mine: The Art of Giving

1. What would you do if you hit the lottery and won a million dollars?

2. What are the world's messages concerning money and riches?

3. How can money change people?

4. Is it possible for a Christian to be rich and still love and obey God? Explain.

5. How can a wealthy Christian be used by God?

6. What tends to keep you from giving as much as you should?

7. How can you begin to increase your giving?

8. Which part of the acronym G-I-V-E do you need to work on the most?

   1. **G**enerously
   2. **I**ndividually
   3. **V**oluntarily
   4. **E**verything without credit

   What can you do about it this week?

Overview

The Radical Forgiveness of God

TOPIC
The forgiveness of God

DESCRIPTION
At some time in our lives all of us have asked the question, *How could God ever love a person like me?* The answer to that question lies in the incredible forgiveness that God has for us. Students today need to get a grasp on the kind of love and forgiveness that are available from God. Once they gain a better understanding of that, they will enter into a deeper, more intimate and life-changing relationship with Him.

KEY VERSE
"'But while he was still a long way off, his father saw him and was filled with compassion for him; he ran to his son, threw his arms around him and kissed him.'" Luke 15:20

BIBLICAL BASIS
Matthew 6:14,15; Luke 15:11-24; John 3:16; 8:2-11; Romans 4:7; 8:38,39; Ephesians 4:32; 1 Peter 1:18,19

THE BIG IDEA
God's love is based on who you are, not what you do!

PREPARATION
- *Runaway Bunny* by Margaret Wise Brown (Harper Torchbooks: New York, 1977)

Be prepared to read the story to the group.

Outline

The Radical Forgiveness of God

INTRODUCTION

Read *Runaway Bunny* by Margaret Wise Brown as an opening illustration about the type of love and forgiveness that God has for you. It's the story of a bunny who decides to run away from its mother, yet no matter where the bunny chooses to run, the mother is right there with open arms and love.[5]

This is a great illustration about the type of love that our heavenly Father has for each of us. No matter where we run, He is always there. Stress the following points:

- God has an incredible love for each of us.
- No matter where you go, no matter what you've done, He comes after you with His incredible love/forgiveness.
- Just as the mother bunny would go to any length to find her child, God feels the same toward us.

> **The Big Idea:** God's love is based on who you are, not what you do!

Today's story is about:
- The incredible forgiveness of God.
- Someone who messed up and feels unforgivable.

It is the "Parable of the Loving Father."

BODY OF THE MESSAGE: RADICAL FORGIVENESS

Read Luke 15:11-24.

I. We're Just Like the Son

   A. We set out for distant land.
   B. Our dreams turn into a nightmare.
   C. We find ourselves in desperate need—at rock bottom.

D. We decide to come back, but with apprehension/fear/doubts. Our reaction: *What will my Father think about me? Will He still love me?*

E. We are welcomed home by the Father.

II. God's Forgiveness Is Radical for Everyone, for Anything, for Anytime.

A. God's love and forgiveness are unconditional—with no strings attached.

B. God's love and forgiveness are complete—the offense is never brought up again (see Romans 4:7).

C. We don't deserve it, but God chooses to give it to us.

D. The father fully restored him as a son!

III. God's Forgiveness Came at a Cost

A. Forgiveness cost Him His only Son—Jesus Christ (see 1 Peter 1:18,19).

B. God knew the cost and was willing to pay it. He couldn't stand to live without you because of His radical love for you (see John 3:16).

C. The father gave the best as a sign of his forgiveness: robe, ring, sandals and fattened calf.

D. There was a high price paid for forgiving you, me, all of us.

IV. God's Forgiveness Calls for a Response

A. It calls for a changed life such as Jesus declared to the woman caught in adultery (see John 8:2-11).

B. What's your response going to be?
   1. Arrogant disobedience
   2. Thankful obedience

C. It also calls us to forgive others in the same way (see Matthew 6:14,15).
   1. We are called to forgive to the same extent as the Father.
   2. We are called to forgive unconditionally and completely.
   3. We are called to pay the price for forgiveness.

CHALLENGE/ACTION STEPS

There are three types of people here today:

1. Some of you need to come home to the Father.
   - You've been out on your own too long—afraid to come home.
   - You'll find Him there, running to you, arms open wide.
   - Come home to the Father.

2. Some of you have business to do with someone else.

- You need to forgive someone with the same radical love and forgiveness that God has shown you.
- Some of you may need to ask someone to forgive you. Do it as soon as possible.
3. Some of you need to respond to His forgiveness.
   - You've never experienced the radical love and forgiveness of Jesus Christ.
   - It's for everyone, anything, anytime—but it came at a great cost.
   - God is offering His hand to you right now.

Read the following story:

The Pardon

In Louisiana, there was a trial that held the attention of the entire state. The year was 1982 and a man was condemned to die for the murder of a family. As he sat on death row, his attorneys frantically tried to secure a pardon for their client.

They used just about every means within their grasp. As the hour approached, all hope seemed to fade. Then unexpectedly, at 11:30 P.M., one half hour before he was to die in the gas chamber, the governor of Louisiana extended a full pardon to the man.

The attorneys were overjoyed as they brought the news to their client. As they told him of his freedom something happened that brought the state of Louisiana to a standstill. He refused the pardon. At precisely 12:00 midnight, they strapped the man to the chair and within a few moments he was dead. The entire state was in shock. The man had a full pardon, yet chose to die anyway.

A fierce legal battle soon erupted over this issue: Was the man pardoned because the governor offered the pardon, or was he pardoned only when he accepted the pardon? The highest court in the state of Louisiana was the arena for the debate. Ultimately it was decided that the pardon cannot go into effect until it is accepted.

So it is with us. God offers us eternal life, a pardon from sin, yet too often we reject the pardon. God offers the pardon, but we need to accept it.[6]

Notes:
5. For more storybook ideas, check out *Fresh Ideas Resource 2: Case Studies, Talk Sheets & Discussion Starters* by Jim Burns and Mark Simone (Ventura, Calif.: Gospel Light, 1997), pp. 97-102.
6. For more illustrations, check out *Fresh Ideas Resource 1: Stories, Illustrations and Quotes to Hang Your Message On* by Jim Burns and Greg McKinnon (Ventura, Calif.: Gospel Light, 1997), pp. 11-207.

The Radical Forgiveness of God

1. What makes God's unconditional love and forgiveness so inviting?

2. Why is it so hard to accept the unconditional love and forgiveness of God?

3. How are we like the prodigal son in the parable?

4. How did the father respond to the son's coming home?

   Was it the expected response?

   What does the father's response say about our heavenly Father?

5. How does it feel to know that the Father has paid the price for you to be forgiven and to return to a relationship with Him?

6. What are some of the areas where you have strayed from the Father in order to "do your own thing"?

7. Read Ephesians 4:32 and Matthew 6:14,15. God calls us to forgive others just as He has forgiven us. Is there someone you need to forgive, just as God forgave you? What will you do about it?

Spend some time in prayer as a group, asking for the incredible, unconditional love of God, as well as making decisions to forgive others to the same degree.

Overview

God's Love Letter to You

TOPIC
The power of applying God's Word in our lives.

DESCRIPTION
God's Word is a love letter to each of us. It's a letter from the heart of the Father to your heart. It's a letter telling you how much He loves you, what He thinks about you, what He dreams about you and what He desires for you. Yet, if we never open it up or read it, we miss out on the blessing and the growth that come from being in the Word. Along with that comes the application of the Word. Students need to apply the Word of God, His love letter, in their lives. Within the pages of the Bible lies the power to transform lives, but it needs to be applied before the change is experienced.

KEY VERSE
"Do not merely listen to the word, and so deceive yourselves. Do what it says."
James 1:22

BIBLICAL BASIS
Joshua 1:8; Psalm 1; 119:9-11,105; John 8:31,32; 15:10,11; 16:33; 17:17; 2 Timothy 3:16,17; James 1:22-25

THE BIG IDEA
God's Word is His love letter to you, but you need to apply it to see results.

PREPARATION
• A bar of soap in original wrapper

Outline

God's Love Letter to You

INTRODUCTION

Irish Spring and the Word of God

Hold up the bar of soap. Ask the question:

How is God's Word like this bar of soap?

Allow your group to reply. Then tell them something like this:

This soap has the power to clean you and remove dirt from your body. Inside this box (or wrapper) is a bar of soap that contains the chemicals needed to clean your body, but as long as they remain in this box (or wrapper), they are useless. For me to release the power of the soap to clean my body, I need to take the bar out of the box (or wrapper) and apply the soap to my body. God's Word is exactly like that.

God's Word has the power to transform your life. It has the power to change your life completely, but as long as it sits unopened the power can never be released. God's Word is living and active and able to change your life, but to release the power you need to apply it. To release the power of God's Word you need to open it up and read it, but most importantly, apply it to your life. Soap is faithful and so is God's Word.[7]

> **The Big Idea:** God's Word is His love letter to you, but you need to apply it to see results.

Here are three ways to apply God's love letter to your life and see the results:

- Read it.
- Remember it.
- Respond to it.

BODY OF THE MESSAGE: RELEASING THE POWER

I. Read God's Word—Joshua 1:8

A. First thing we need to do is crack open the cover. Sometimes that's the toughest thing to do.

B. Be encouraged to meditate—be in the Word—every day.

C. Three ingredients for daily meditating on the Word:
1. Time: When will you spend time reading?
Choose a consistent time during the day—morning or evening.
2. Territory: Where will you spend time reading?
Get away from distractions.
3. Translation: What will you read?
Get a Bible translation you can understand. The *NIV Student Bible* is a great one to use.

D. The place to start is by making the time to open God's Word and sticking to it!

II. Remember God's Word—Psalm 119:11

A. More than just reading, we need to reflect on it!
We need to think about what it says and ask the question, What does it mean for *my* life?

B. Hiding the Word in your heart:
1. Treasure the Word.
2. Think about the Word.
3. Memorize the Word.

C. As you spend time reflecting on God's Word, it will transform your way of thinking and seeing things around you. You will see things from a different perspective—God's.

D. The Holy Spirit who lives inside you will bring it back to memory.

E. As you think about and reflect on it, God will speak to you.

III. Respond to God's Word—James 1:22-25

A. There's more than just reading; more than just reflecting and remembering it—we need to put into action what we find within the pages.

B. Like soap, the power of God's Word is only released when we apply what we are reading—i.e., "do what it says."
1. Example One: A person sees himself in a mirror, walks away, forgets.
2. Example Two: A person who looks into the mirror intently, acts on what he sees; will be blessed/happy (true joy and fulfillment in life).

C. Truly happy people are those who study God's Word. They don't forget what they have read, but they do something about it— they apply it.

D. Which one will you be? Will you act upon what you read?

CHALLENGE/ACTION STEPS

Repeat The Big Idea:

> **The Big Idea:** God's Word is His love letter to you, but you need to apply it to see results.

- Read it!—Set a time and territory and select a translation.
- Remember it!—Reflect on what you're reading.
- Respond to it!—Apply it, do something with what you've read and heard.

Note:

7. For more object lessons, check out *Fresh Ideas Resource 2: Case Studies, Talk Sheets & Discussion Starters* by Jim Burns and Mark Simone (Ventura, Calif.: Gospel Light, 1997), pp. 55-69.

God's Love Letter to You

1. Why do you think God gave us the Bible?

2. Why is it difficult for most people to spend time reading the Bible?

3. What do you think are some of the advantages of reading the Bible?

4. Read the following passages.
   What are the benefits and/or promises concerning reading God's love letter regularly that are found in the following verses?

   Joshua 1:8

   Psalm 1

   Psalm 119:9-11

   Psalm 119:105

   John 8:31,32

   John 15:10,11

   John 16:33

John 17:17

2 Timothy 3:15-17

CHALLENGE/APPLICATION

What keeps you from spending time—or more time—in God's Word?

What is one thing that impacted you from this lesson?

What will you do about it this week?

How can we, as a small group, keep one another accountable for reading, remembering and responding to God's Word?

Overview

No Thanks, I'd Rather Be Ungrateful!

TOPIC
Thankfulness

DESCRIPTION
Thankfulness is a lost art today. Just as parents long to hear the words "thank you" from their children, so our heavenly Father loves to hear thankfulness from our mouths and hearts. This message focuses on developing a habitually thankful attitude toward God and His blessings for us.

KEY VERSE
"Give thanks in all circumstances, for this is God's will for you in Christ Jesus."
1 Thessalonians 5:18

BIBLICAL BASIS
Psalm 100:1-5; 107:1; Luke 17:11-19; Romans 5:8; Colossians 3:15-17; 1 Thessalonians 5:18

THE BIG IDEA
Thankfulness is an attitude of gratitude for all that God has given to us.

PREPARATION
For Introduction:
- Video camera and blank cassette
- VCR and TV

Before the meeting, interview a few of your students giving their answers to the following question on the video: What is one thing you are thankful for and why? Record their responses. Prepare to show the video during the Introduction.

For Body of the Message:
- A copy of *Did I Ever Tell You How Lucky You Are?* by Dr. Seuss (Random House Books for Young Readers, 1973).

Prepare to read the story to the group during the message.

Outline

No Thanks, I'd Rather Be Ungrateful!

INTRODUCTION

Video Interviews

Show the video interviews you have previously taped as a way to begin the message on thankfulness. Make the following observations:

- We live in a world that lacks happiness and true joy.
- Happiness and true joy can only be found in being thankful.
- What keeps us from being thankful people?

Today, I want to challenge each of us to be more thankful.

BODY OF THE MESSAGE : KEYS TO THANKFULNESS

I. Thankfulness Is an Attitude

A. The "When..., then..." game
  - "When I get _____, then I'll be happy."
  - "When I _____, then I'll really feel significant."
B. Thankfulness is an attitude that you choose to have.
C. "Give thanks in all circumstances" (1 Thessalonians 5:18).
  - Not *for* all circumstances, but *in* all circumstances
  - "Thank God no matter what happens" (1 Thessalonians 5:18, *The Message*).
D. Thankfulness is the way that you look at things, a new perspective.

Read *Did I Ever Tell You How Lucky You Are?* by Dr. Seuss after introducing it by saying the following:

No matter who you are or what you've been through, thankfulness is an attitude of the heart. This story illustrates thankfulness as only Dr. Seuss can.[8]

E. Thankfulness is an attitude, choosing to be thankful!

II. Thankfulness Is a Habit

A. Read 1 Thessalonians 5:18 again:
  1. "For this is God's will for you in Christ Jesus."
  2. "This is the way God wants you who belong to Christ Jesus to live" (*The Message*).
B. God is calling us to be a people of thankfulness.
C. We need to develop a lifestyle of habitual thankfulness.
  1. Habit (according to *Webster's Dictionary*) is "an involuntary pattern of behavior acquired by frequent repetition; a manner of conducting oneself; an addiction."
  2. "Frequent repetition"—continual choice to be thankful.
  3. "Manner of conducting oneself"—lifestyle of thankfulness.
D. A habit of thankfulness will transform your life from being a cynical, hard person to being a grateful one.
  1. Habitual thankfulness changes your perspective on life.
  2. It starts with an attitude and with frequent choices to be thankful.

III. Thankfulness Is a Response

A. Thankfulness is born out of a gratitude for what God has done for you.
B. Psalm 100:1-5 and Psalm 107:1 tell us God has been good to each of us!
C. God has given us so much:
  1. Give examples.
  2. Romans 5:8 says that most of all God has given us salvation through His Son!
D. We have so much to be thankful for. The problem is that we don't take the time to look for or acknowledge our blessings!
E. Your thankfulness should be born out of all the things that God has given you and done for you.

IV. Thankfulness Is an Action

A. More than all that, thankfulness is something that we need to do something about.
B. Just like the grateful leper in Luke 17:11-19, our thankfulness should drive us to action! Don't be like the 10, but be like the one who came back to give thanks!

REVIEW

- Attitude
- Habit
- Response
- Action

> **The Big Idea:** Thankfulness is an attitude of gratitude for all that God has given to us.

CHALLENGE/ACTION STEPS

Being a Person of Thanks: "Hey, Thanks!"

Have students write out things that they are personally thankful for. Have them take the list home, put it up somewhere where they will see it and remember to thank God for the things they have listed.

I AM THANKFUL

Write down what you are thankful for, using the acrostic below (be creative!):

T _____

H _____

A _____

N _____

K _____

F _____

U _____

L _____

N _____

E _____

S _____

S _____

"Give thanks in all circumstances, for this is God's will for you in Christ Jesus."
1 Thessalonians 5:18

Note:

8. For more storybook ideas, check out *Fresh Ideas Resource 2: Case Studies, Talk Sheets & Discussion Starters* by Jim Burns and Mark Simone (Ventura, Calif.: Gospel Light, 1997), pp. 97-102.

No Thanks, I'd Rather Be Ungrateful!

Read 1 Thessalonians 5:18 and answer the following questions:

1. Why is it difficult to have an attitude of thankfulness?

2. What are a few reasons why thankful people are happier people?

3. How do you think it makes God feel when we are thankful?

   When we complain?

Thankfulness Brainstorm

We often miss the things that we should be thankful for. Come up with a list of at least 20 things that your group members are thankful for. Do more than 20 if your group thinks of 20 things quickly. Have someone act as secretary and write down the list and read it back when you are finished.

Overview

I've Changed My Mind

TOPIC
Guarding your mind

DESCRIPTION
Our minds are battle zones where Satan tries to gain control by sending missiles of negative thoughts and information to distract and destroy us. The things we allow into our minds affect everything we do. The battle is raging and this message will help equip students for the battles they face every day.

KEY VERSE
"Above all else, guard your heart, for it is the wellspring of life." Proverbs 4:23

BIBLICAL BASIS
Proverbs 4:23; Matthew 12:34; Romans 12:1,2; Philippians 4:8

THE BIG IDEA
What you put into your mind radically affects what comes out in the way you live your life.

PREPARATION
For Introduction:
- Blender
- Extension cord
- Vanilla ice cream
- Milk
- Chocolate syrup
- Large cups
- Serving spoon
- Sardines or a fish from the grocery store
- Spinach
- Clam juice
- Any other unpalatable items you can think of

Set the blender on a table or other flat surface where everyone can see it, and plug it in. Have all of the ingredients nearby.

For Challenge/Action Steps:
- 3x5-inch index cards
- Pens or pencils

Outline

I've Changed My Mind

INTRODUCTION

I've Changed My Mind

Here's a great way to visually illustrate the idea of garbage in, garbage out and the principle of Philippians 4:8. Begin by talking about the things that we put into our minds and how they affect us. This is an illustration in two parts.

For the first part, make a chocolate milk shake using the vanilla ice cream, milk and chocolate syrup. After making the milk shake, pour the shake into a few cups and give to a few students in the group. Talk about the ingredients you've put into the blender to make the milk shake. The delicious ingredients you put into the blender affected what came out of the blender—the chocolate milk shake.

For the second part of the illustration, make another milk shake with the vanilla ice cream, milk, chocolate syrup, and then begin to add the rest of the listed items. As you add the rest of the items, talk about the garbage we sometimes put into our minds—pornography, vulgar music, terrible movies, etc. As you finish with your concoction, ask if anyone would like to have a milk shake now.

Draw the following parallels:

- What you put into your mind affects what comes out.
- What you put into your mind comes out and affects how others view you. (Remember how no one wanted the second batch of milk shakes!)
- Discuss Philippians 4:8 and the things that we need to be filling our minds with.[9]

Explain:

1. We are bombarded with messages every day that have an effect on us.
   - Advertising: The major focus of advertising today is on young people.
   - Television and movies: Affect our values and our views concerning "normal" life and sexuality.
   - Music: The messages and themes in music also affect our values.

2. What you allow into your mind has an influence on you.

- Your heart: values, attitudes, beliefs about life
- Your tongue: what you say and how you say it (see Matthew 12:34)
- Your actions: influence your attitude and the choices you make

> **The Big Idea:** What you put into your mind radically affects what comes out in the way you live your life.

Today I challenge you to examine your mind and what you allow into it.

BODY OF THE MESSAGE: THREE KEYS TO CLEANING YOUR MIND

I. Key One: Guard Your Mind

A. God's Word challenges us to guard our hearts/minds (see Proverbs 4:23).
B. We need to be conscious of what we put into our minds.
C. Remember the blender illustration: Guard the ingredients that go into your mind to control what comes out.
D. The first step is to evaluate what you put into your mind. Ask yourself:
  1. What do I dwell on?
  2. What do I allow into my mind?
  3. What are the values? What are the messages?
  4. Do they honor Christ?
  5. What are the effects on my life?

II. Key Two: Fill Your Mind

A. We need to take responsibility for what we allow into our minds.
B. Philippians 4:8 is God's prescription for your mind—The P-E-R-T P-L-A-N:

Pure	Praiseworthy
Excellent	Lovely
Right	Admirable
True	Noble

  1. We need to dwell on these things!
  2. What are you choosing to fill your mind with?
  3. We need to take action to program our minds with the PERT PLAN.

III. Key Three: Renew Your Mind

A. Romans 12:1,2 is a call to renew our minds!
B. We need to continually fill our minds to renew them.
  1. Fill our minds with God's love letter and the PERT PLAN.

2. We need to renew daily, consistently and habitually.
3. Only then will we be able to keep our minds and thoughts pure.

CHALLENGE/ACTION STEPS

What you dwell on and allow into your mind will affect you!
We need to choose what we do and do not allow into our minds.

Guard your mind.
Fill your mind according to the P-E-R-T P-L-A-N.
Renew your mind.
- Your mind will be transformed.
- Your heart and attitude will be changed.
- You will gain control over your tongue.
- Your life will be utterly transformed!

Reflection

Give a 3x5-inch index card and a pen or pencil to each student. On one side of the card have them write down Proverbs 4:23. On the other side, have each of them write down something that influences their minds in negative ways. Have them keep their cards as reminders of the key verse and the areas they need to work on.

Note:
9. For more object lessons, check out *Fresh Ideas Resource 2: Case Studies, Talk Sheets & Discussion Starters* by Jim Burns and Mark Simone (Ventura, Calif.: Gospel Light, 1997), pp. 55-69.

I've Changed My Mind

1. What are some of the messages we get bombarded with every day?

   Where do the messages come from?

2. Why is it difficult to guard your mind?

3. What are some of the consequences of not guarding your mind?

4. What are some of the benefits of guarding your mind?

5. What are some of the ways you can fill your mind?

   What should you fill your mind with?

6. What do you need to do this week to help guard your mind?

Overview

Knowing You're Not Alone

TOPIC
Dealing with the issue of loneliness in our lives

DESCRIPTION
Loneliness is an issue that a lot of students are dealing with. You probably can easily think of a time when you felt lonely. Loneliness is something that all students will deal with at some point in their lives. It's not a case of *if*, but *when*. This message examines the issue of loneliness and what we can do to combat loneliness in our lives.

KEY VERSE
"The LORD is my shepherd, I shall not be in want." Psalm 23:1

BIBLICAL BASIS
Deuteronomy 31:8; Psalm 23; 25:16-18; Mark 14:31,50; Hebrews 10:24,25

THE BIG IDEA
All of us will experience loneliness at some point in our lives. Jesus knows your heart and will be with you during those times.

PREPARATION
For Introduction Option One:
You will need to find someone (student or adult) to prepare a monologue on loneliness.
For Introduction Option Two:
- Video clip from EDGE TV on Loneliness: Edition 4 (EDGE TV c/o IMS Productions, 530 Communication Circle, Suite 206, Colorado Springs, CO 80905, Phone 800-726-7285 or edgetv_orders@imsproductions.com, www.edgetv.com)
- VCR and TV

Set up the TV and VCR to show the video clip from EDGE TV on Loneliness: Edition 4.

Outline

Knowing You're Not Alone

INTRODUCTION

Option One: Drama/Sketch on Loneliness

If you have someone in your group who is great at speaking/drama, have them put together a monologue about the issue of loneliness. Have them discuss what it's like to be lonely, either with themselves, some other person not onstage, or with God. To conclude, have "God" make an offstage reply to the person onstage about His understanding and presence during lonely times.

Option Two: Loneliness from EDGE TV

Use the video clip from EDGE TV on Loneliness (Edition 4). Show the clip—almost 11 minutes long—or if that is too long, find a segment that is appropriate for getting students to think about the issue of loneliness. Stress the following:

Loneliness is a feeling a lot of you are dealing with:
- Question Number One: Where do I belong?
- Question Number Two: Where do I fit in?
- Question Number Three: Who really cares for me and what I'm going through?

BODY OF THE MESSAGE: KNOWING YOU'RE NOT ALONE

I. Loneliness Is Normal

A. Everyone feels lonely at times. It's normal and natural.
B. You are not alone in dealing with this issue—though you may feel like it!
  1. The 90s is the decade of loneliness!
  2. You are members of the loneliest generation ever!
C. We need to deal with loneliness—prolonged loneliness leads to depression.

II. Loneliness Is More Than Being Alone

A. You can be lonely in a crowd—it's more than just being alone.
B. It's a feeling of being an outcast or outsider.
  1. Lack of value/significance: *Do I really matter?*
  2. Lack of purpose: *Do I really have a purpose in life?*
  3. Lack of a support system: *Is there anyone who really cares about me?*

III. Jesus Knows What It's Like to Be Lonely

A. Read Mark 14:31,50.
B. Jesus knows what it feels like to be deserted and lonely.
  1. He sees and cares!
  2. The people He needed the most, trusted the most, all deserted Him!

IV. Working Through Loneliness

A. Don't withdraw.
  1. Withdrawal is our first impulse. *Don't*; keep in touch!
  2. Isolating yourself only makes it worse.
  3. Don't medicate your loneliness with drugs, sex, food, TV, video games, bad relationships, etc.
  4. We need each other (see Hebrews 10:24,25).
B. Depend on God.
  1. Reach out to God in the midst of your loneliness.
  2. Read Psalm 23 and 25:16-18.
  3. Tell Him what you're feeling. He really cares!
  4. He is always there for you, whether you feel it or not.
  5. He will always believe in you, your significance and value.
  6. When lonely times come, go to God with your loneliness.
C. Develop special friendships.
  1. Reach out to others instead of pulling back.
  2. Cultivate special friendships:
    • People you can rely on during lonely times;
    • People who genuinely care for you, value you, accept you;
    • People who give you a support system in those times of need.
  3. Reach out and serve others. Be others centered.
  4. One of the best things you can do to work through loneliness is to take your eyes off yourself and place them on others.
D. Devise a P-L-A-N for when you feel lonely.
  1. **P** = Prayer: Seek God in prayer; bring your feelings to Him—He cares!
  2. **L** = Lean on others: That's what friends are for!

- Who could you seek out? You need to cultivate friendships.
- You need a sense of belonging and the support of others.
    3. **A** = Activities: What could you do or get involved in?
- Something to restore your feeling of value and significance
- Something that restores your feeling of purpose
- Give examples from your own life:

    4. **N** = New experiences
- Try something new with others.
- Build memories that will help you through the tough times.

CHALLENGE/ACTION STEPS
Feeling lonely? It's normal! But don't just let it continue.

Review

1. Don't withdraw.
2. Depend on God.
3. Develop special friendships.
4. Devise a plan:
    Prayer
    Lean on Others
    Activities
    New Experiences

Knowing You're Not Alone

1. Some experts say that you are the loneliest generation ever. Do you agree? Why or why not?

2. How can loneliness be destructive?

   How can it be constructive?

3. How does knowing that Jesus was also lonely at times help and encourage you?

4. How can relationships impact your loneliness?

5. Complete the following sentences:

   I'm the most lonely when...

   I wouldn't get so lonely if I could just...

   You could help me when I'm lonely by...

6. What are some things you can do to work through loneliness in your life? Think about relationships and activities that might help.

   What action will you take in the next two weeks to do something about it?

Overview

Falling in Love with Jesus

TOPIC
Loving God

DESCRIPTION
We were created to have a relationship with God, but what type of relationship? It's not a relationship built on rules and regulations, but something more. It's not built by a religion or a system of beliefs, but something more. Our relationship with God needs to be based on love. God desires that we enter into a love relationship with Him. This message encourages students to move beyond the rules of religion and into a life-changing love relationship with their God.

KEY VERSE
"Love the Lord your God with all your heart and with all your soul and with all your mind and with all your strength." Mark 12:30

BIBLICAL BASIS
Matthew 11:29,30; Mark 12:30; Romans 5:8; 1 John 3:16-18; 4:7-21

THE BIG IDEA
Christianity is a life-changing love relationship with God.

Outline

Falling in Love with Jesus

INTRODUCTION

Getting What You Don't Deserve

Father Maximilian Kolbe was a Catholic priest sentenced to be imprisoned in Auschwitz in May 1941. Upon his arrival at Auschwitz, he was informed that the life expectancy of a priest was about a month in Auschwitz. Father Kolbe took it upon himself to be an agent of love within the dismal hopelessness of the barbed-wire fences.

One night in July 1941, amidst the sounds of motorcycles and barking dogs, a man from Barrack 14 escaped from Auschwitz. The next morning as the prisoners lined up for morning role call, they noticed the gallows in front of them—empty. The escapee had succeeded, yet someone would pay the price for him. That morning, 10 men were "selected" to die in the starvation bunker inside "The Death Block." One of those men was Number 5659. As the ten were being led away to the screams of horror, a small, frail frame stepped forward. His number was 16670. His name was Father Maximilian Kolbe.

"Sir, I'd like to die in place of one of those men."

"In whose place do you want to die?" asked the Commander.

"For that one." Father Kolbe lifted his finger and pointed at Number 5659. And in an instant, Number 5659 was erased from the death ledger and Number 16670 was entered. One life for another—a gift of life. On August 14, 1941, in a starvation bunker known only as Cell Number 21, in the basement of Barrack Number 11, one man gave a gift of life by dying in place of another. Number 16670 died in place of Number 5659.

It was a cold, overcast day when another man gave His life. Light in the darkness, love afloat in the middle of a sea of hate, hope in the midst of madness. On that hill, Jesus gave His life for all mankind, but not only all mankind, but for you and me. A gift of life and an act of love, given because of God's incredible love for you and me.

"Sir, I'd like to die in the place of one of those men," He said.

"In whose place do you want to die?"

"For that one."

Just as Father Maximilian Kolbe, 16670, gave the gift of life to prisoner 5659, so Jesus

Christ has given us the gift of life and of grace. For just as prisoner 5659 experienced a radical grace, a gift that was never deserved—so do we experience a gift that we do not deserve: the amazing grace and forgiveness of God.[10] Christianity isn't a religion, but a relationship with a loving God! Christianity isn't about a bunch of rules, it's about falling in love with Someone who is crazy about you.

> **The Big Idea:** Christianity is a life-changing love relationship with God.

God is absolutely crazy about you—God's Word is His love letter to you.

What does it really mean to fall in love with Jesus?

BODY OF THE MESSAGE

I. Letting Him Have It All—Mark 12:30

  A. Falling in love with Jesus is more than just an emotion.
  B. Falling in love with Jesus means committing all of your life to Him.
  C. It means allowing Him into those areas of your life that are tough for you.
  D. The Jewish *Shema*[11] is recited every day. It's a daily decision.
  E. It's not a checklist, but rather shows that commitment is one that encompasses all of who you are.
    Ask:

What are some of the things that stand between you and your love for Jesus?

Mark 12:30 tells us that we should love Jesus with all that we have and are.

II. Listening and Obeying His Voice—1 John 5:2,3

  A. Falling in love with Jesus is not about following rules—a list of dos and don'ts.
  B. Falling in love with Jesus means hearing His voice and following Him.
  C. In a guy/girl relationship you'll do anything for that person, just because you love him or her! The difference between before and after you have fallen in love? A change of heart and focus.
  D. God's commandments are not burdensome when you love Him!
    1. Is following God a burden? Check your love for Him!
    2. Have you heard His voice lately?
  E. If you're fully in love with Jesus, following Him will be a joy.
    1. Hungering/seeking after Him will be a joy.

2. Living a life of love becomes our delight, not a burden. His burden will be light (see Matthew 11:29,30).

3. God's commands will bring freedom—the liberty that we want so badly!

III. Loving Others—1 John 4:7-21

A. Falling in love with Jesus also means loving others.

B. God is inviting us to love others as He loves them—with the same quality of love and to the same extent.

1. How does God love us? Completely and unconditionally!

2. We are called to express the same love for others.

C. First John 4:19-21 is a warning for us! Do you really love Him or not?

1. You only love God as much as you love the person you love the least.

2. Loving God is lived out in how you love the people around you.
- Jesus acted on His love for you (see Romans 5:8).
- Love is a decision and is shown in action (see 1 John 3:16-18).

3. Loving God is loving people as Jesus would, no matter who they are or what they've done (unconditionally, like Father Maximilian Kolbe).

4. Are you loving others? It shows the state of your love for God.

CHALLENGE/ACTION STEPS

Where is your love relationship with Jesus today?

- He longs to enter into a love relationship with you.
- God loves you with an incredible love.
- Crawl up into the lap of God; call Him "Daddy." It's His greatest joy!
- No matter where you are or what you've done, His love for you remains the same.
- He's calling to you, "Love me because I love you, and not for any other reason."
- You don't have a relationship? All you have to do is fall in love with Jesus. Come to Him today!
- Do you already have a relationship? Love Him!
  1. What area of your life do you need to give to Him today?
  2. Do you have joy in following Him?
  3. Show your love for God by how you love others.

Note:
10. Mike DeVries, *The Word on the New Testament* (Ventura, Calif.: Gospel Light, 1996), pp. 97-98.
11. *Shema* is the Jewish confession of faith made up of Deuteronomy 6:4-9; 11:13-21; Numbers 15:37-41.

Falling in Love with Jesus

1. Complete the following sentences:

   • I think having a relationship with God means...

   • When I think about what it means to love God, I think of...

   • I felt closest to God when...

2. What are some things that come between us and our love for God?

3. Why do God's commands seem so burdensome at times?

   If we love God, why won't His commandments seem so burdensome?

4. How does loving others show our love for God?

5. Which of the following phrases describes your love for God today? Explain why:

   ❑ White Hot?   ❑ Cooling Off?
   ❑ Warming Up?   ❑ Living in the Antarctic?
   ❑ Smoldering?

6. In which of the following three areas do you need to work on falling in love with Jesus more?

   ❑ Letting Him have it all
   ❑ Listening and obeying His voice
   ❑ Loving others

7. What will you do to work on that area?

Overview

Seen and Not Heard

TOPIC
Loving one another

DESCRIPTION
When Jesus was asked what the most important commandment was, He replied that it was to love God with all that we are and to love others as ourselves. One of the hardest things to do as a Christian is to love others, especially those who are not like us. Yet, in God's Word we are called to love everyone, just as Jesus loves. This message guides students to discover what it takes to love those around us just as Jesus loves them.

KEY VERSE
"The second is this: 'Love your neighbor as yourself.' There is no commandment greater than these." Mark 12:31

BIBLICAL BASIS
Mark 12:31; Luke 10:30-37; John 13:34,35; Romans 13:8; Philippians 2:4; James 2:15-17; 1 John 3:16-18

THE BIG IDEA
Our love for others needs to be seen, not just heard!

PREPARATION
For Introduction Option One:
Gather and/or make the following props for the melodrama:
- A "Jerusalem—5 miles or so" sign
- A "Jericho—down 3 miles to the left" sign
- Two tree branches for the person who plays the tree
- A "Tree" sign for the tree
- A glass of water

- A "Harry's Roadside Hotel—1 mile" sign and someone in audience to throw it onstage
- A welcome mat

For Introduction Option Two:

- *Veggie Tales* video: "Who Is My Neighbor?"
- VCR and TV

Cue the video to begin at the correct spot.

Outline

Seen and Not Heard

INTRODUCTION

Option One: "The Adventures of Mr. Good Guy and Mr. Happy Traveler"

A melodrama loosely based on Luke 10:30-37.

Prepare the props beforehand and have them available.

Select 10 people to be a part of this melodrama. Be sure to select people who feel comfortable doing some pretty outrageous things in front of the group.

After you have selected the students and assigned the characters, have them stand "offstage" until they are read into the scene. Be sure to remind them that the more creative and outgoing they are, the better the melodrama will be. The key to a good melodrama is pausing and emphasizing when you need to, so take a few minutes to read over the melodrama before you read it to the group. You may also want to personalize it a little, by adding or adapting jokes to your group (include any inside jokes your group may have).

"THE ADVENTURES OF MR. GOOD GUY AND MR. HAPPY TRAVELER"

Characters:

Mr. Happy Traveler
One tree
Three thugs
One pastor
One church leader from the First Church of Jericho
Mr. Good Guy
Buck, the donkey
Harry, the innkeeper
(Onstage is the lone tree, holding two branches and a sign that says "Tree," and two signs, one pointing toward Jerusalem and the other pointing toward Jericho.)

One very fine day, a man was traveling along the roadside, minding his own business, singing a happy tune. He was a very fine singer. The audience applauded. Mr. Happy

Traveler took a bow.

Since it was early in the morning, Mr. Happy Traveler was stretching and doing deep knee bends while he continued to sing.

All of a sudden, peering from behind the tree were three of the meanest, toughest, most ruthless thugs in all the land. As they sneered and flexed from behind the tree, each one looking more mean and nasty than the other, the thugs had a disagreement and began to fight among themselves.

Mr. Happy Traveler heard the noise. He stopped his singing and deep knee bends and said, "Harketh, who goeth thereth?" Just then the thugs froze with peculiar smiles on their faces. Mr. Happy Traveler began singing a happy tune again.

Quietly, the thugs crept up on Mr. Happy Traveler and jumped him, beating him senseless (well, almost senseless). After the thugs had done their deed, they stood up, leaving Mr. Happy Traveler in a heap on the floor, just smiling now instead of singing. They looked around in amazement as the voice of the narrator said, "Now that you've beaten Mr. Happy Traveler, what are you going to do next?"

"We're gonna go to Disneyland!" they proclaimed as they exited, leaping and skipping from the stage.

As Mr. Happy Traveler lay groaning on the floor *(let Mr. Happy Traveler groan for a while)*, along came the pastor from the local church, whistling a praise song. The pastor was so oblivious to Mr. Happy Traveler that he tripped over him. The pastor apologized. Mr. Happy Traveler groaned, "That's okay."

The pastor knelt down near Mr. Happy Traveler to see if he was still alive. He checked his pulse. The pastor jumped to his feet and proclaimed, "He's alive! He's alive! He's alive!!!" Bending over, the pastor asked Mr. Happy Traveler, "Pardon me, do you know how I can get to the First Church of Jerusalem? I'm late, I'm late, for a very important date!" The audience groaned because it was a dumb joke. Mr. Happy Traveler groaned and pointed to the sign. The pastor thanked him and left for Jerusalem, whistling another praise song.

As Mr. Happy Traveler lay groaning again only this time louder (let Mr. Happy Traveler groan for a longer time), along came a leader of the First Church of Jericho, hurrying along and mumbling to himself. Without knowing it, the church leader tripped over Mr. Happy Traveler. Scrambling to his feet, the church leader apologized. Mr. Happy Traveler groaned, "That's okay."

The church leader, noticing that Mr. Happy Traveler needed some help, began to quote verses from the Bible to comfort Mr. Happy Traveler *(let the church leader go on for a little while)*. After exhausting all the verses he knew and looking around for some help, the church leader began to sing "Kum-ba-ya." The audience joined in. The church leader, feeling proud for a job well done, patted himself on the back. The audience stopped singing the annoying song. The church leader bent over Mr. Happy Traveler and said, "Yea verily, verily I beseech thee. *(pause)* Couldst thou tell me where I might find

the Jerusalem 7-11? With all this singing, I'm dying for a Big Gulp!" The audience in unison pointed toward Jerusalem. The church leader thanked the audience and exited toward Jerusalem saying, "Oh, thank heaven for 7-11!"

As Mr. Happy Traveler lay groaning for a third time, this time even louder, along came Mr. Good Guy and his sidekick, Buck the donkey. The audience applauded loudly. Now, Mr. Good Guy was watching where he was walking and did not trip over Mr. Happy Traveler. Mr. Happy Traveler thanked Mr. Good Guy. "You're welcome," replied Mr. Good Guy.

Mr. Good Guy bent down over Mr. Happy Traveler. He had pity and compassion on him, saying, "Poor Mr. Happy Traveler." The audience mimicked, "Poor Mr. Happy Traveler." He took Traveler's pulse and poured water on him. Then picking up Mr. Happy Traveler with a grunt, Mr. Good Guy placed Mr. Happy Traveler ever so gently on his trusted donkey, Buck. Buck groaned *(pause)* and said, "I hate this job." Buck and Mr. Good Guy then ventured high and low in search of the local inn. "I know what we need," cried Mr. Good Guy. "A sign." *("Harry's Roadside Hotel—1 mile" sign is thrown from the audience onto the stage.)* The audience groaned because it was yet another dumb joke.

Going farther, they met Harry the Innkeeper, who was holding out the welcome mat (Harry holds the welcome mat). Harry said, "Hello, Mr. Good Guy. Hello, Buck. Who's the guy with the smile on his face?"

"This is Mr. Happy Traveler," said Mr. Good Guy, waving Mr. Happy Traveler's hand. "Could you look after him for me and if he needs anything, put it on my American Express Card; I never leave home without it." Mr. Good Guy placed Mr. Happy Traveler ever so gently on the doorstep of Harry's Roadside Hotel, and with his best Arnold Schwarzeneggar impersonation, said, "I'll be back!"

As Mr. Good Guy and Buck turned to take off into the sunset, Harry the Innkeeper exclaimed, "What a good guy!" The audience joined in, "What a good guy!" And all the people said "The end!"[12]

Note:
12. Mike DeVries, *The Word on the New Testament* (Ventura, Calif.: Gospel Light, 1996) pp. 32-34.

Option Two: *Veggie Tales:* "Who Is My Neighbor?"

Use the video clip from *Veggie Tales:* "Who Is My Neighbor?" This is an excellent parable take-off of Luke 10:30-37. It's a great way to get your students into the topic!

Discuss the following question:

What does it mean to love one another?

Love is more than just saying something to get what you want, or doing something for what you'll get in return.

Mark 12:31 tells us to "love your neighbor as yourself."

> **The Big Idea:** Our love for others needs to be seen, not just heard!

Today we'll look at what it truly means to love one another.

BODY OF THE MESSAGE

I. Love Is a Responsibility

Read John 13:34,35.
- A. We are called to love one another—with no parameters and unconditionally.
- B. "Love as I have loved you." We are called to love like Jesus has loved us.
  - 1. For example: Little League batters want to bat just like their hero, going through all the same motions. They watch their hero bat and try to be just like him.
  - 2. We need to watch how Jesus loved to be able to love like He did.
- C. Believers' love for one another demonstrates God's love (see v. 35). Love is demonstrated in our actions, not just our words.
- D. You are responsible for loving one another!

II. Love Is a Debt We Owe

Read Romans 13:8.
- A. We always have one outstanding debt: We are always to be in debt to one another—a debt of love.
- B. We are in debt to Christ for all that He's done for us.
- C. We repay our debt of love by loving others.
- D. You only love Jesus as much as the person you love the least.

III. Love Is an Action

Read 1 John 3:16-18.
A. Love needs to be an *action*, seen and not just heard!
B. Our love for Christ needs to move us to action in loving others.
C. Living out your love for others expresses your love for God.
D. Love is shown even in the small things.

> **The Big Idea:** Our love for others needs to be seen, not just heard!

CHALLENGE/ACTION STEPS

1. Break out of your comfort zone.
   Step outside of what's comfortable for you.
   It starts with a decision!
2. Reach out to those around you. Reach out with:
   • Genuine Concern—really care about what's going on.
   • Genuine Care—offer honest support and love.
   • Genuine Commitment—to one another and to putting love into action.
3. Reach out to others here. Within our group, there are people who are hurting and in need of your active love!
4. Reach out to others you know. If this group has impacted you, invite someone else to be a part of it!
5. Live out your love in action.
   a. Ways to live it out here in our group:
      • Welcoming everyone
      • Introducing yourself to others
      • Building others up
      • Caring for others
   b. Ways to live it outside our group:
      • Showing genuine care and concern by serving others
      • Meeting needs
      • Living out the love of Jesus Christ

Review

> **The Big Idea:** Our love for others needs to be seen, not just heard!

Seen and Not Heard

1. What do you think it means to love one another as God loves you (see John 13:34)?

   How has God lived out His love for us?

2. What are some roadblocks to loving one another?

   Why does it seem so tough?

3. Read Philippians 2:4. We are called to look out for the interests of others. What keeps us from living out that verse?

4. Read James 2:15-17 and 1 John 3:16-18. What do these passages say about loving others?

   What can we do to put our love into action?

5. Who in your life right now needs love?

   What will you do for this person that will put your love into action?

6. What was one thing that you heard in this message that impacted you?

   What will you do to make that be a part of your life?

Overview

What Happened to You?

TOPIC
What happened when you became a Christian

DESCRIPTION
When you become a Christian, there is a transformation that takes place. It's a transformation into a new life. That transformation holds the key to what it means to be a Christian, live for Christ, relate with other believers and see yourself as God sees you. This message explains what took place the moment we started a relationship with Jesus Christ.

   Note: If you have children, this is a great message to add illustrations, pictures, videos, etc., of your growing children to help you in explaining new life in Christ.

KEY VERSE
"Yet to all who received him, to those who believed in his name, he gave the right to become children of God." John 1:12

BIBLICAL BASIS
John 1:12; 3:1-21; Romans 8:12-17,38,39; 1 Corinthians 12:12,13; 2 Corinthians 5:17; 1 Peter 2:9,10

THE BIG IDEA
Becoming a Christian means starting a new life.

PREPARATION
For Introduction Option One:
* *Children's Letters to God*, compiled by Stuart Hample and Eric Marshall (Workman Publishing, 1991), or letters or prayers written by children in your own congregation

Prepare to read a few letters from *Children's Letters to God*, compiled by Stuart Hample and Eric Marshall, or any other book with children's letters to God. **Option:** You could instead have children from your church write a letter to God or a prayer that can have the same effect.

For Introduction Option Two:
• A copy of the video *Look Who's Talking* (1989, Tri-Star Pictures, Inc.)
Cue the video of *Look Who's Talking*, showing the introduction to the movie—the "inside" view of conception.

Outline

What Happened to You?

INTRODUCTION

Children are a gift from God; they teach us a lot about spiritual things: trust, faith, honesty, creativity, imagination, inquisitiveness.

Option One: *Children's Letters to God*

Read a few children's letters to God (from the book or from children in the congregation) as an introduction to the message. You could also have children from your church write you a letter or a prayer that can have the same effect.

Explain and discuss the following:

- When someone becomes a Christian, they begin a new life as a child of God (see John 1:12).
- When you think of a child or a new life, what comes to mind (i.e., innocent, delicate, blank slate, impressionable; teachable; total dependency; needs instruction, guidance and protection; vision for the child's future; etc.)?

Option Two: *Look Who's Talking* Video Clip

Show the introduction to *Look Who's Talking*, depicting the "inside" view of conception. It's a funny clip that will draw your students into the topic of new life and birth.

Explain:

That's the natural process of producing a new life, but today we want to look at the spiritual process of producing "new life"—what happens when you become a Christian.

> **The Big Idea:** Becoming a Christian means starting a new life.

BODY OF THE MESSAGE: WHAT HAPPENED TO YOU?

Read John 3:1-21—Nicodemus's conversation with Jesus is a story about new life!

- Being born again
- God initiated the whole process by sending Jesus Christ
- The transformation/life change that comes from new life

I. New Life Means a New Birth

A. Being a Christian starts with being born again.

B. Children go from the warm, cozy environment of their mother's womb into a cold, harsh outside world.

C. That's total transformation. You are totally different/new; you can't go back!

D. The old has gone, new has come, you're a new creation (see 2 Corinthians 5:17)!

   1. You are reconciled—in a new relationship with God.

   2. You have peace with God—no longer His enemy.

   3. You are no longer in relationship with sin, but now in relationship with God.

E. "New birth" means a completely different way of life; not an addition to your life, but a transformation.

II. New Life Means a New Identity

A. Being a Christian means having a new identity through our relationship with God.

B. It's not a new set of rules to keep, but a new relationship.

C. It's not getting something new, but *being* something new!

D. "New identity" means a new relationship with God.

   1. You can call God "Daddy" (see Romans 8:15).

     • He is a loving Father. His love is based on who you are, not on what you do.

     • Romans 8:38,39 describes a love that knows no end.

   2. You now have intimacy with God—spend time with your Creator.

   3. You have access to God. You can pray to Him, come to Him anytime, anywhere, about anything—He always has the "Open" sign on.

   4. God calls the shots—let Him be the boss!

     Not only are you born again, you now have a new relationship based on love.

III. New Life Means a New Title

A. Being a Christian means you have a new title and position.

B. You've been changed—changing your title shows what's happened.

C. First Peter 2:9,10 explains this new title:

1. Chosen people, royal priesthood, holy nation, people belonging to God.

2. You are now a child of God (a son or daughter of the King).

IV. New Life Means a New Family

A. Being a Christian means having a new family.

B. When you became a Christian, you became a part of the family of God.

C. Read 1 Corinthians 12:12,13.

1. God created us to need each other.

2. As a Christian, you are a part of a new family that has the same relationship with God that you do.

D. As Christians, we have a responsibility to one another in the family.

1. Everybody belongs.

2. Everybody is cared for.

E. "New family" means you are part of a larger body—the Church, the Body of Christ. Being a Christian means:

1. Having others who share your relationship with God;

2. Sharing the same journey;

3. Needing one another;

4. Encouraging one another.

CHALLENGE/ACTION STEPS

> **The Big Idea:** Becoming a Christian means starting a new life.

- Live like a Christian, and if you're not already a Christian, you can start a relationship with God right now.

- **Optional:** Give each student a piece of paper, an envelope and a pen or pencil. Have them write letters to God, thanking Him for what He's done for them in creating new life within them. They could write the letters to themselves from God's perspective, telling what they've learned about new life in Christ. Mail the letters back to students within the next month or so.

What Happened to You?

1.   What are some of the similarities between physical birth and spiritual birth?

2.   How would you answer Nicodemus's question in John 3:4,9?

3.   What does it mean to have a new life in Christ?

4a. How does it feel to know that you are...

     Chosen by God?

     A Royal Priesthood—interceding for man before the Lord?

     A Holy Nation—belonging to the kingdom of God?

     Belonging to God—a treasure, not a possession?

4b. What do those things look like today?

5.   Read Romans 8:12-17. As a Christian, you have an incredibly intimate relationship with God—you can call Him "Daddy." How does that impact your everyday life?

6.   Which aspect of new life is the toughest for you to see in your own life?

7.   What can we do this week, as a group and as individuals, to live out the new life we have in Christ?

Overview

Me, Myself and I

TOPIC
Selfishness and self-centeredness

DESCRIPTION
Self-centeredness is a disease that impacts all of us. Our world is billed as a consumer world, one that is always asking the question *What's in it for me?* Self-centeredness is a disease that turns our eyes inward, shutting off other people, their concerns and their needs. Yet in our search for true happiness, we find it lies not in being self-centered, but in being others-centered. This message deals with the issue of self-centeredness and how to get our eyes off ourselves and onto others.

KEY VERSE
"Do nothing out of selfish ambition or vain conceit, but in humility consider others better than yourselves." Philippians 2:3

BIBLICAL BASIS
Jeremiah 9:23,24; Matthew 6:24; 20:26-28; 23:12; Romans 12:1,2; Philippians 2:3,4; James 4:6,10

THE BIG IDEA
True happiness and joy come from being God-centered and others-advancing, rather than being self-centered.

PREPARATION
• *Yertle the Turtle & Other Stories* by Dr. Seuss, storybook or video (New York: Random House Books for Young Readers, 1966)

Outline

Me, Myself and I

INTRODUCTION

Make the following points:

- Self-centeredness is a disease that affects your relationships with others and God.
- Self-centeredness is a disease that turns your eyes inward to who *you* are, what *you've* done, what *you* want, what *your* dreams are.
- Self-centeredness is a disease that consumes and destroys your life.

Yertle the Turtle

Yertle the Turtle focuses on the issue of status and what we'll do to others to get it.[13] Read the story (or show the video) to your group and make the following comments:

- "Nothing's higher than ME!" That's the cry of self-centeredness.
- Yet in the end, it's Yertle's self-centeredness that leads to his downfall.
- So it is with us; self-centeredness is our downfall.

> **The Big Idea:** True happiness and joy come from being God-centered and others-advancing, rather than being self-centered.

Explain:

- When we try to please ourselves, there's never any satisfaction!
- We always want more, to be better, to gain more success, etc.
- To be truly happy in life takes getting our eyes off ourselves and onto God and others around us.

Today we will look at what it takes to get rid of self-centeredness.

BODY OF THE MESSAGE

I. Self-Centered or God-Centered?—Matthew 6:24

A. Ultimately, we do everything for one of two reasons: to serve ourselves or to serve God.

B. We do things either to bring us glory and honor or to bring God glory and honor.

C. We do things either to make ourselves look good or to please God.

D. Self-centered = focus on what it takes to make ourselves look good/success.

E. God-centered = focus on making God the recipient of glory/honor.

II. Self-Advancing or Others-Advancing?—Philippians 2:3,4

A. Are you looking out for yourself only? What will it take to get ahead?

B. Are you looking out for what it will take to help others succeed, even if it comes at a cost to you?

III. Three Antidotes for Self-Centeredness

A. Give God your heart—Romans 12:1
  1. Offer your heart to God as a daily, living sacrifice (daily decision).
  2. Giving God your heart means:
     a. Giving Him your dreams, goals, desires, and asking for His plan!
     b. Seeking Him with all your heart—to know Him and love Him more.

Do you daily give God control of your life, heart, circumstances?

  3. Giving Him your heart will cure you of focusing on yourself!
B. Give God your humility—James 4:6,10
  1. God loves the humble, but hates the proud.
  2. People who are prideful are glory thieves saying: "Look at me!"
  3. Humility focuses the glory back where it belongs—on God!
  4. He's the one who has given us gifts, talents, abilities—not we ourselves!
  5. Humility means having an accurate view of ourselves and God.
  6. Humility is a process of growth—it takes time to gain an accurate view of self and God.
C. Give God your hands—Matthew 20:26-28
  1. If you want to cure self-centeredness, focus on serving others!
  2. You're never more like Jesus than when you serve!
  3. Focusing on the needs of others...
     a. Takes your eyes off yourself.
     b. Gives you a proper perspective on life (seeing others' needs).

c. Gives you true fulfillment and joy.
4. Jesus' advice was that if you want to be first then learn to be a servant.
   a. Being a servant means being aware of those around you.
   b. Being a servant means being willing to do something about the needs of others.

CHALLENGE/ACTION STEPS

- We live in a self-centered world—focused on self and self-advancement.
- God's call is to be different—to be God-centered and others-advancing.
- If you're looking for true happiness and joy, that's where it's found!

Action Steps for the Week: Set the P–A–C–E

P = **P**rideful or humble—which are you?
A = **A**dmit any areas of self-centeredness to God.
C = **C**hoose to give your heart, humility and hands to God.
E = **E**xpress your servanthood to someone this week.

Note:
13. For more storybook or video clip ideas, check out *Fresh Ideas Resource 2: Case Studies, Talk Sheets & Discussion Starters* by Jim Burns and Mark Simone (Ventura, Calif.: Gospel Light, 1997), pp. 97-113.

Me, Myself and I

1. Why is our world so self-centered or self-focused?

2. Why is it tough to take our eyes off ourselves and put them on others?

3 How can being others-centered lead to true happiness?

4. How would you define the word "humility"?

5. Who in your world would you describe as "others-centered"?

   What makes them others-centered?

6. What is your biggest roadblock to being others-centered?

7. What can you, or we as a group, do this week to become more others-centered?

Overview

The Apple of His Eye

TOPIC
The basis of our self-image

DESCRIPTION
Self-worth and self-identity are two of the biggest issues facing students. How we answer the questions *Who am I?* and *Am I really significant?* will say a lot about the lives we lead, the depth of our walk with Christ and the struggles that we face in our lives. This message delves deeper into the issues that shape our views of who we are and how God views us.

KEY VERSE
"For we are God's workmanship, created in Christ Jesus to do good works, which God prepared in advance for us to do." Ephesians 2:10

BIBLICAL BASIS
Psalm 139:1-4,13-18; Zechariah 2:8; Romans 8:15,16,35-39; Ephesians 2:8-10; 1 Peter 1:18,19; 1 John 3:1

THE BIG IDEA
God's love is based on who you are, not on what you do!

PREPARATION
For Option One Introduction:
- A roll of aluminum foil

For Option Two Introduction:
- "Gertrude McFuzz" by Dr. Seuss—a story from the book *Yertle the Turtle & Other Stories* (New York: Random House Books for Young People, 1966)

Outline

The Apple of His Eye

INTRODUCTION

Option One: Foil Mask

Have four volunteers come up front. Give each volunteer a large piece of aluminum foil. Give them a few minutes to make masks of their faces using the aluminum foil, then use the masks as visual aids while making the following observations:

- Each of us is uniquely created.
- Yet too often we hide behind masks because we don't like what we see!
- We use masks to become who we think we should be!
- The sad thing is that the masks are all hollow *(crumple up a mask)*.
- Masks represent our search for significance. Give examples of masks that students wear to hide or find significance—i.e., cool dude, tough guy, class clown, beauty queen, the jock, etc.

Option Two: "Gertrude McFuzz"

"Gertrude McFuzz" is a wonderful story that focuses on comparing ourselves to one another and coming up short—what we will do to seem better than others and finally realizing that being ourselves isn't that bad after all.[14]

Read the story to your group and make the following comments:

- We compare ourselves to others in order to feel significant and to find love, acceptance and worth. We try to mold ourselves into the likeness of those we admire.
- The sad thing is that we end up being the loser. We lose our uniqueness!
- There are four things that we usually base worth/significance on:

> Beauty: how we look.
> Brains: our intellect, grades, position in life.
> Bucks: money, materialism, what we have.
> Brawn: our athletic abilities, performances.

- Don't base your self-worth on things that are temporary and fragile. In the midst of all those voices, God's voice gets drowned out!

> **The Big Idea:** God's love is based on who you are, not on what you do!

Today, we look into God's love letter to you and discover what He thinks about you!
Psalm 139:1-4,13-18 says that God does think about you.

BODY OF THE MESSAGE

I. You Are Loved

A. You are loved by God. He's crazy about you!
B. God's love for you is based on who you are, not on what you do!
C. Read Romans 8:38,39. There is nothing that you can do to make God stop loving you!
   1. There is nothing in your past or the present.
   2. No sin or mistake will make Him love you any less!
D. God's love is...
   1. Unconditional—with no strings attached
   2. Constant—never changing from day to day, year to year
   3. Forever—has absolutely no end

II. You Are Unique

A. Like the foil masks, you are a unique creation of God.
B. There is no one exactly like you. God made you exactly the way you are!
C. Ephesians 2:10 says you are God's workmanship—handcrafted by Him.
D. Remember: when you look in the mirror, God sees eternal perfection! What do *you* see?
E. You are a unique child of the living God!

III. You Are Valuable

A. You are valuable to God, not for anything you do, but for who you are!
B. All of us have priceless treasures for which we...
   1. Are willing to pay any price.
   2. Have a passion for taking care of it.
   3. Assign great value.
   4. Give places of honor.

C. You are God's priceless treasure!
   1. Zechariah 2:8 says you are the "apple of His eye."
   2. First Peter 1:18,19 says you were bought with a precious price.
D. Your picture is in God's office and wallet—you are valued!

IV. You Are Gifted

A. As a Christian, God has gifted you to do incredible things for Him. Maybe these things are not going to make the news, but they will impact eternity!
B. Ephesians 2:10 says you are created in Christ Jesus to do good works.
C. God has already been dreaming of the things that He wants to do through you.
D. As a Christian, God has gifted you with a unique ministry to others through your…
   1. Spiritual gifts;
   2. Special talents and abilities.
E. God values you enough that He has given thought to your gifts, talents and abilities. He has given them to you for a purpose.

CHALLENGE/ACTION STEPS

• Don't fall for the Four *B*s—beauty, brains, bucks and brawn! You are worth more than what's on the outside!

> **The Big Idea:** God's love is based on who you are, not on what you do!

• You are loved, unique, valuable and gifted!
   1. Believe it.
   2. Live it.
      • Live for Christ. Put Him first in all you do—which is your response of love for Him.
      • Live up to your potential. Be who you are!
      • Use your giftedness.

Note:
14. For more storybook ideas, check out *Fresh Ideas Resource 2: Case Studies, Talk Sheets & Discussion Starters* by Jim Burns and Mark Simone (Ventura, Calif.: Gospel Light, 1997), pp. 97-102.

The Apple of His Eye

1. Why do people seek love, acceptance and significance?

2. How does the world define love, acceptance and significance?

   How does God define it?

3. In what ways do you see people searching for significance through the Four *Bs*?

4. Which of the Four *Bs* is the toughest area for you in your search for significance?

5. How do the following verses apply to your life in your search for significance?

   Romans 8:15,16

   Romans 8:35-39

   Ephesians 2:8-10

   1 John 3:1

6. Which of the following four areas is the toughest for you to understand and see in your own life: Being loved, unique, valuable or gifted?

7. When was a time that someone loved you unconditionally? What happened?

   How did you feel?

8. Why do many people have a hard time accepting God's unconditional love in their lives?

9. What is one thing that you heard in this message that impacted you?

   How will you be different because of hearing this message?

Overview

Improving Your Serve

TOPIC
Servanthood

DESCRIPTION
We live in a world that defines "greatness" as having it all, winning the game, being Number One. In God's economy, greatness means being a servant. Those who desire to be great need to be servants. This message focuses on what it takes to improve our service to others.

KEY VERSE
"Not so with you. Instead, whoever wants to become great among you must be your servant, and whoever wants to be first must be slave of all." Mark 10:43,44

BIBLICAL BASIS
Mark 10:43-45; John 13:1-17; 1 John 3:16-18

THE BIG IDEA
If you want to do something that has eternal significance and give your life meaning, be a servant because being great means being a servant!

PREPARATION
For Introduction Option One:
• A video clip of a championship-winning moment
Before the meeting, secure a copy of any sporting event that has a celebration feel to it.
For Introduction Option Two:
• Collect items that represent greatness and servanthood. For example:

Greatness Symbols	Servanthood Symbols
a trophy	cleaning supplies
money	a basin of water with towel
a car	a mop and bucket

Arrange the collected Greatness and Servanthood Symbols on a table at the front of the room.

For Challenge/Action Steps:

• Several used dishtowels

Before the meeting, cut the dishtowels into small strips (approximately one inch wide and eight to ten inches long) to be given out at the end of the message as reminders to be servants.

Outline

Improving Your Serve

INTRODUCTION
Stress the following points:

- Most of us, if we were honest, would want to be served, not to serve!
- Serving/servanthood is the complete opposite of what we think of when we consider greatness.
- The world defines being great as having it all, winning the game, being important, successful and/or influential.

Option One: Championship Video Clip

Show the video to help students see how the world defines greatness.

Option Two: Greatness or Servanthood Illustration

Hold up each item as you describe how the world defines "greatness" or how God defines "greatness."

Greatness Symbols	Servanthood Symbols
a trophy	cleaning supplies
money	a basin of water with towel
a car	a mop and bucket

Option Three: Random Acts of Servanthood

This is a great impromptu way of getting students to experience how easy being a servant can be. Divide the whole group into smaller groups of five or six. Give the groups 10 minutes to complete an act of servanthood. It could be for another group, the house you're meeting in, the church you're at or for complete strangers in the neighborhood.

When the groups come back, have them report on what they did as their act of servanthood. Make the following observations:

- Servanthood is easy if you have the motivation and mind-set.
- Servanthood can be the simple things that we do for others.

I want to give you another view—Jesus' view of greatness! Mark 10:43-45 tells us that greatness means being a servant.

> **The Big Idea:** If you want to do something that has eternal significance and gives your life meaning, be a servant because being great means being a servant!

Setting the Scene: Jesus' Example

Read John 13:1-17. Make the following points:

- The disciples had just finished arguing about who was the greatest among them. Jesus teaches them a lesson they will never forget.
- Explain the custom of foot washing.
- Jesus gives them an example to follow.
- Jesus' hope is that the disciples would pick up on the example and live it!

BODY OF THE MESSAGE : IMPROVING YOUR SERVE

I. Putting Others First

A. One of the biggest keys to improving your serve is to seek to put others first.
B. However, we live in a me-focused world. When it really comes down to it, we're looking out for our interests most of the time.
   1. We wonder why we are so unhappy, why we lack true joy.
   2. We're so wrapped up in ourselves—what others think, what we need to do next to get ahead.
   3. We get so caught up in the world's mind-set that we lose our joy and lose sight of others.
C. To truly be great, to be a servant, we need to open our eyes to the needs and interests of others.
D. In the midst of His last evening before being killed, Jesus focused on the needs of His disciples and demonstrated His concern by cleaning their feet.

Are you looking out for yourself or are you looking out for others?

II. Putting Aside Your Pride

    A. Pride is the enemy of servanthood.
        1. Pride says, "I'm too good for _____!" or "I'm too important/influential. My time is better spent doing _____!"
        2. If we truly want to be great in the eyes of Jesus, we need to be servants, to set aside our pride.
    B. Jesus, the Son of God, set aside His own needs to do the lowest of all tasks—washing feet! He took off His outer garments, wrapped Himself in a towel and performed the most menial task in the world.

   Is there any task that you think is "beneath" you?

    C. Improving your serve means setting aside your pride and taking the attitude that says, "I'll do anything, anytime, anywhere because of what Jesus did for me!"

III. Putting It into Action

    A. Improving your serve means being willing to get your hands dirty.
    B. More than just talking about it, servanthood is action!
    C. Jesus didn't tell them about what it meant to be great—He showed them!
    D. Jesus didn't talk about being a servant—He took off His clothes, put on a towel and served!

   Who in your life needs to be served: friend, parent, girlfriend, boyfriend, brother, sister, neighbor?

    E. The most important question is *So what will I do about it?*
    F. Love and serving is an action, not words (see 1 John 3:16-18)!

CHALLENGE/ACTION STEPS

Being a servant is as easy as A-B-C:

    A—**A**sk God to make you a servant (every day this week).
    B—**B**e open to opportunities to serve (keep your eyes/ears open).
    C—**C**ommit to action: Make a "hit list" of people that you want to serve. Choose five people and five acts of servanthood to do this week.

If you're up for a challenge, make an agreement with your group to serve together. Maybe you can serve in one of the areas listed under question 4 of the Discussion Starters on page 112, or find other areas in which your group can serve together.

This is a great opportunity to make a difference and build relationships with your group. If at all possible, take the challenge! Remember, the best ideas for service projects are ones that the students come up with themselves. So let them dream a little—they'll surprise you!

Servant Symbols

Before your meeting, obtain several used dishtowels. Cut them into small strips (approximately one inch wide and eight to ten inches long). Give a piece of towel to every student as reminders to be servants this week. Suggest that they put them in a prominent place such as on their key chains, where they can see them and be reminded of their call to be servants.

Improving Your Serve

1. Why do you think it is so hard to serve others?

2. Should we go on serving and caring for someone when there is little or no response from them? Why or why not?

3. Which of the following is the toughest for you when it comes to serving from your heart, and why?

   Putting others first

   Putting aside your pride

   Putting service into action

4. What can you and/or our youth group do to serve:

   Your family?

   Your friends?

   Your school?

   Our church?

   Our community?

5. On the back of this page, list some ideas for people or groups that we can serve together.

6. Share your ideas from your hit list of five people to serve and five ways to serve this week.

Overview

Handling the Heat: This Pressure Is Killing Me!

TOPIC
Handling sexual temptation

DESCRIPTION
One of the biggest struggles students encounter is how to handle their hormones and their emotions. Students hear so much about sex and sexuality. There are so many mixed messages flying around today, no wonder they have a hard time figuring out what the truth about sex is. This message addresses the issue of handling the heat and surviving the pressures in a sex-crazed world!

KEY VERSE
"No temptation has seized you except what is common to man. And God is faithful; he will not let you be tempted beyond what you can bear. But when you are tempted, he will also provide a way out so that you can stand up under it." 1 Corinthians 10:13

BIBLICAL BASIS
2 Samuel 11; 12:1-13; Proverbs 6:27-29; John 8:1-11; 1 Corinthians 6:18-20; 10:13; 13:4-7; Galatians 5:16; Ephesians 5:3-6; 1 Thessalonians 4:3-8

THE BIG IDEA
The choices you make today will impact you for the rest of your life.

PREPARATION
Gather the following simple costumes and props:
- Four bedsheets
- Four pillowcases
- A bathrobe
- Binoculars
- Small plastic wading pool

Outline

Handling the Heat: This Pressure Is Killing Me!

INTRODUCTION

David and Bathsheba

To illustrate how not to deal with temptation, recreate the story of David and Bathsheba from 2 Samuel 11:1-5 and 12:1-13, showing the wrong way to deal with temptation. You'll need six actors to portray the following characters:
David
Bathsheba
Nathan
Two guards
A person offstage as the "voice of God"

Invite volunteers up front and give them simple costumes.

- For David, Nathan and the guards, give actors bedsheets to wrap themselves up in and pillowcases for headwear.
- For Bathsheba, provide a bathrobe to wear over her clothes.
- Also give David a pair of binoculars with which to spy on Bathsheba.
- Have Bathsheba bathe in her bathrobe in a small plastic wading pool.
- Use your imagination to include any other props that add interest to the story.

As you read through the story, have the actors act out their parts and lines. Encourage them to ham it up as much as possible. After the drama, stress the following points:

How to Handle the Heat/Pressure

- It's great that God created sex/our sex drive—now what?!

- How to handle this out-of-control sex drive:
  1. Pray that the feeling goes away?
  2. "Just Say No!"?
  3. Give in?
- Handling sexuality can be tough—I know!

> **The Big Idea:** The choices you make today will impact you for the rest of your life.

Read Ephesians 5:3-6; Proverbs 6:27-29; Galatians 5:16.

It all comes down to choices and consequences.
There are some pretty serious consequences to being sexually active:
- Physical: STDs, pregnancy
- Emotional: guilt, being used, anger, bitterness, fear, etc.
- Relational: a warped view of love that will impact your future marriage

God says to wait until marriage for this most incredible experience because He loves you and wants to protect you from needless pain and suffering!

BODY OF THE MESSAGE: SURVIVING THE PRESSURE AND HANDLING THE HEAT

I. Set Your Sights

A. You need to set your sights on what you will and will not do.
B. "Flee sexual temptation" (see 1 Corinthians 6:18).
  1. You need to make a decision. Look at the consequences and decide.
  2. Not to decide *is* to decide. Don't wait until you find yourself at "Perspiration Point"!

II. Set Your Standards

A. How far can I go? It's an important question that is asked a lot.
B. How far should I go?—Better question to ask! You need to set your limits now.
C. Does God's Word tell us how far is too far? Not really!
D. What the Bible *does* say:
  1. Read 1 Corinthians 6:19,20.
     a. Honoring God with our bodies requires radical respect.
     b. How do you honor God with your body?
  2. Read 1 Thessalonians 4:3-8.
     a. Are you in control or not?

   b. Are you taking advantage of the other person to satisfy your own desires?

  3. Read 1 Corinthians 13:4-7.

   a. Is what you're feeling true love or just true lust?

   b. Do you love others, especially when you are dating, in the way that is described in this passage?

 E. It's essential that you set your standards, both individually and as a couple, at the beginning of a relationship. It'll keep you out of trouble!

III. Analyze Your Situations

 A. Read 2 Samuel 11. David was in the wrong place at the wrong time!

  1. We need to look at the situations we fall into.

  2. We need to avoid long periods of idleness. Keep busy.

 B. How do you handle the heat?

  1. Talk about it with your boyfriend/girlfriend.

  2. Avoid the "hot spots"—the places and situations that make it difficult to keep your standards.

  3. Get rid of the three Ms—There's more to creative dating than McDonald's, movies and making out!

  4. Lean on God (see 1 Corinthians 10:13).

IV. Take the Second Chance

 A. Maybe you're wondering: *What if I've already blown it? Is there forgiveness?* You bet!

  1. Read John 8:1-11 (especially vv. 10,11). Jesus told the woman caught in adultery: "Neither do I condemn you....Go now and leave your life of sin."

  2. Jesus doesn't condemn her. He offers her freedom and forgiveness and calls her to change her lifestyle.

 B. If that's you, take the second chance that Jesus is offering you!

CHALLENGE/ACTION STEPS

- God created sex, and He created you and your sex drive!
- How do you handle the heat and survive the pressure?

 Sights
 Standards
 Situations
 Second Chances

> **The Big Idea:** The choices you make today will impact you for the rest of your life.

Handling the Heat: This Pressure Is Killing Me!

Agree or Disagree

Read through the following statements. Let students vote whether they agree or disagree with the statements. Interact with students and their opinions. Use this time as a launching pad into the discussion on the issue of handling sexual temptation.

1. Agree/Disagree   If you really love the person, it's okay to be involved sexually.
2. Agree/Disagree   Sexuality is a human need.
3. Agree/Disagree   Handling sexual feelings and pressures is hard.
4. Agree/Disagree   It's easier to give in than not to.
5. Agree/Disagree   This is an area that I struggle with.

Questions

1. Why do you think teens feel so much pressure to have sex?

2. What are some ways teens react to the pressure to have sex?

3. Why is it (or isn't it) difficult to deal with the pressure to be sexually involved?

4. If you had a friend who came to you and told you that he or she was thinking about being sexually involved with his or her boyfriend/girlfriend, what would you tell him or her?

5. What would you do if you had a Christian friend who you knew was sexually active? What would you say or do?

   What if you have a non-Christian friend who is sexually active? What would you say or do?

6. Which of the four *Ss* could you identify with the most? Which impacted you the most?

   • Sights (see 1 Corinthians 6:18)

   • Standards (see 1 Corinthians 6:19,20; 1 Thessalonians 4:3-6; 1 Corinthians 13:4-7)

   • Situations

   • Second chances (see John 8:1-11)

7. What do you need to do to handle the heat of being sexually involved?

Overview

Being a Ficus for God

TOPIC
Growing spiritually

DESCRIPTION
God's desire for each of us as Christians is that we grow in our walk with Him. It's like marriage—one day we begin that new relationship, yet we need to tend to that relationship every day to help it grow and flourish. This message focuses on our need to care for our relationship with God to help it flourish!

KEY VERSE
"Not that I have already obtained all this, or have already been made perfect, but I press on to take hold of that for which Christ Jesus took hold of me." Philippians 3:12

BIBLICAL BASIS
1 Corinthians 9:24,25; Philippians 3:10-16; Colossians 1:28; 3:1-17

THE BIG IDEA
Growing spiritually requires a daily desire and decision to be devoted to Christ.

PREPARATION
For Introduction:
Before the meeting, you'll need to purchase or secure the following items:
- A small house plant
- A small pot for the plant
- Plant food (Miracle Gro, or some other variety of food)
- Potting soil
- A glass of water
- Gardening trowel, gloves and apron (for the dramatic effect!)

For Challenge/Action Steps:
- Purchase seeds—large ones (i.e., peas and beans) that students can keep, enough for one for each student

Outline

Being a Ficus for God

INTRODUCTION

Here's a way to challenge your students toward deeper growth in their relationship with God.

Begin by stating some comparisons between the plant and the Christian life—e.g., we receive Christ and begin our journey as a small seed that begins to blossom into a plant, but to continue in our walk with Christ we need to grow.

Ask group members what it would take for the plant to grow properly. As they discuss some of the things the plant needs in order to grow, begin repotting the plant in front of the group, explaining each step and the importance of each item or ingredient in the process. Talk about the following items:

- For the plant to grow, we need to take action by caring for it, just as we must with our walk with Christ.
- Each ingredient we use in repotting the plant is essential for its growth, just as there are ingredients that are essential in helping our relationship with Jesus grow, such as reading His Word, prayer, fellowship, worship, spiritual disciplines, etc.
- Just as we may not see the growth in this plant from day to day, over time you see the fruits of growth. So it is with our relationship with God. You may not see growth every day, but over time you'll see growth and its fruit!
- When we begin to "outgrow" our environment (e.g., become complacent and comfortable), we need to be "repotted" (e.g., challenged with a new step of maturity). If we don't move into a new experience, we may become stunted or cease to grow spiritually altogether.

The following outline summarizes the process of growth:
1. SEED IT—begin your relationship with God.
2. FEED IT—take action by caring for your relationship with God every day.
3. WEED IT—take time to weed out the areas of your life that need to change.[15]

> **The Big Idea:** Growing spiritually requires a daily desire and decision to be devoted to Christ.

BODY OF THE MESSAGE
Let's see what God's Word has to say about spiritual growth.
Read Philippians 3:10-16.

I. Growing Spiritually Is a Desire (Philippians 3:10)

A. The beginning of spiritual growth is to have a passion and desire to grow and know Christ in a deeper way. People are passionate about a lot of things.

What are some examples of things people are passionate about?

B. Passion means having:
   1. Deep love—deeply valuing/caring for something or someone
   2. Deep sacrifice—willing to do anything
   3. Deep involvement—moving you to action
C. Share what your own passions are.
D. Is God your passion?
   1. Do you have a passion to know Him?
   2. Do you have a passion to live as Jesus would?
E. Having a passion is the beginning of growing spiritually.

II. Growing Spiritually Is a Daily Decision (Philippians 3:12,13)

A. Growing spiritually requires a decision of the will, a decision you make daily.
B. "Press on," "straining forward" means a daily decision.
   1. The Christian life is a marathon, not a sprint.
   2. The Christian life is a process of growth—not instant perfection. That is good news for some of us!
C. Spiritual growth is an intentional process and decision to develop your relationship with God.
D. Spiritual growth is tested by decisions made to follow God with all our hearts whether in easy times or tough times.

Running Illustration:
- Requires a daily decision to get out of bed, put on the shoes and go!
- The decision is made regardless of how you feel, and because of the goal!

Plant Illustration:
- You need to care for it daily, whether you feel like it or not.
- If you let it go (ignore it), it will eventually die.

Good Health Illustration:
- You need to take in God's Word (equivalent to eating right).
- You need to exercise the spiritual disciplines of prayer, worship and living out your faith (equivalent to exercising regularly).

E. We need to choose daily to do the things that will help us grow.

III. Growing Spiritually Is Being Devoted to Christ (Philippians 3:14-16)

A. The goal of spiritual growth is to know Him more and to love Him more.
B. "To win the prize..."
   1. To be more like Jesus—Colossians 1:28
   2. To live up to our calling—Philippians 3:16
C. Make the choice every day to run the race to win the prize—devoting yourself to the goal: becoming more like Jesus Himself (see 1 Corinthians 9:24,25).

CHALLENGE/ACTION STEPS

> **The Big Idea:** Growing spiritually requires a daily desire and decision to be devoted to Christ.

Want to start growing spiritually?
1. Is God your passion/desire?
2. Make a daily decision to grow:
   - Spend time in God's Word, prayer, worship, fellowship.
   - Get involved in a Bible study with others.
3. Seek the goal of being devoted to Christ with all your heart.

Plant illustration—revisited:
- Don't neglect your spiritual life and leave it out to die!
- Seeds for students: Give out a seed (that you previously purchased) to each student in your group as a reminder of the message and the need to care for the seed of his or her spiritual life.

Note:
15. For more object lessons, check out *Fresh Ideas Resource 2: Case Studies, Talk Sheets & Discussion Starters* by Jim Burns and Mark Simone (Ventura, Calif.: Gospel Light, 1997), pp. 55-69.

Being a Ficus for God

1. Where and when was a time that God seemed especially close?

2. Where and when was a time that God seemed especially far away?

3. When it comes to your spiritual life, is it more like...

   ❏ An elevator?
   ❏ An escalator?
   ❏ A roller coaster?
   ❏ A conveyor belt?

4. Read Philippians 3:10-16 together as a group. What are some of Paul's attitudes toward spiritual growth in this passage?

5. Read Colossians 3:1-17. Discuss the following:

   • What spiritual growth principles can you find together in this passage?

   • List the attributes of the new nature found in verses 12-17.

   • How did Jesus model these attributes?

6. What do you think are some of the ingredients it takes to grow spiritually?

7. What are some things that hinder spiritual growth? What encourages it?

8. If someone is feeling spiritually dry and they say they feel far from God, what advice would you give them?

9. What areas of spiritual growth do you need to work on this week?

What will you do about it this week?

Overview

All Stressed Out and No Place to Go!

TOPIC
Stress and worry

DESCRIPTION
One of the hallmarks of teenagers today can be encapsulated in the words "stress" and "worry." Students are professional worriers. If you listen to them talk, you can hear it. This message is designed to help you reach students with the message that stress and worry will rob them of true peace in life.

KEY VERSE
"Therefore do not worry about tomorrow, for tomorrow will worry about itself. Each day has enough trouble of its own." Matthew 6:34

BIBLICAL BASIS
Matthew 6:25-34; Philippians 4:6-8; 1 Peter 5:7

THE BIG IDEA
Worry and stress take our focus off God and rob us of experiencing true peace in our lives.

PREPARATION
- A video camera and blank cassette
- A VCR and TV

Before the meeting, interview several students from the group about the issue of worry and stress. Ask them to respond to the following questions:

1. What is it that you worry about the most and why?
2. What causes you the most stress and why?

Record their responses on videotape and show the video to introduce the topic of worry and stress to your group.

Outline

All Stressed Out and No Place to Go!

INTRODUCTION

How to Worry: Most of Us Don't Need Any Help!

Read aloud the following statements about worry. Add any others that you can think of. The point is to get your students to laugh a little about the things we all might worry about.

Do you worry…

- That if you kiss too much, you'll get mononucleosis?
- That in a long kiss, you'll have to breath through your nose and your nose will be stopped up?
- That you'll get your braces locked during a kiss?
- About dislodging someone's retainer during a kiss?
- That your breath smells?
- That your date's breath smells?
- That you have B.O. and your friends will notice?
- That if you're a girl you won't have any breasts?
- That if you're a guy you *will* have them?
- That your nose is too fat or that your nose is too long?
- That your neck is too fat?
- That your ears stick out?
- That your eyebrows are too far apart?
- That you have one continuous eyebrow?
- If you're a guy, that you'll never be able to grow a mustache?
- If you're a girl, that you *will* have a mustache?
- That you won't like the food at other people's houses?
- That you will eat too much food at other people's houses?
- That when you go to the bathroom, people will hear?
- That the lock on the bathroom door doesn't work?
- That someone will walk in?
- That when you go to the bathroom, you'll run out of toilet paper?

Video Interviews: "What Do You Worry About and Why?"

Show the video interviews.

- Worry and stress are things we all have to deal with.
- A lot of adults don't think your world is *that* stress filled.
- The worry and stress you face is incredibly intense—more than any other generation has faced.
- Stress and worry are real, frustrating, tiring, painful.
- Stress can either bury you or boost you!

Stress can lead to worry, depression, or worse,
OR
It can produce growth in your life.

Will you let stress or worry control you,
OR
Will you search out creative solutions for dealing with stress?

BODY OF THE MESSAGE: ANTIDOTE FOR WORRY

Read Matthew 6:25-34.

I. Get a Proper Perspective (Matthew 6:25-32)

A. Eighty percent of all the things we worry about never happen.
B. A majority of the things that we worry about are things that are tied to the past.
C. We need to remember that yesterday is gone. There is nothing we can do about it.
D. Matthew 6:27 tells us that the things we worry about so often are things that are beyond our control.
E. Verses 26 and 30 are the key: God's antidote for worry is trust in Him.
F. Do you want to begin to handle stress and worry? Begin to realize:
1. Worry doesn't help.
2. God's antidote for worry is trust.

II. Put God First in Every Area of Your Life (Matthew 6:33)

A. Seek God's kingdom first.

B. Shifting our focus off of God and onto the problems is a sure formula for worry.

C. We allow worries and problems to become bigger priorities than God.

D. When that happens, the things we worry about begin to consume us!

E. It's easy to put God on a back burner—put off our relationship with Him.
   - When we're too busy for God, we're busier than He intended for us to be.
   - Set priorities; put God first.

"Your heavenly Father already knows perfectly well that you need them, and he will give them to you if you give him first place in your life and live as he wants you to." (Matthew 6:32,33, *TLB*)

III. Take One Day at a Time (Matthew 6:34)

A. When life's hassles get too big and you feel overwhelmed, stop, take a deep breath and focus on what God is doing today.

B. When you worry about tomorrow, you're worrying about what you can never control, and you rob yourself of peace today.

C. When you begin to worry, stop and refocus on today only. If you can't do anything about it, let it go!

Give your entire attention to what God is doing right now, and don't get worked up about what may or may not happen tomorrow. God will help you deal with whatever hard things come up when the time comes. (Matthew 6:34, *The Message*)

IV. Turn Everything Over to God

A. No matter what comes your way when you begin to worry, take everything to God.

B. God knows what you're going through, how you feel. He cares (see 1 Peter 5:7)!

C. When you begin to worry, don't panic—pray (see Philippians 4:6-8)!
   1. When you come to Him in prayer, you can hand over your worries to the One who has all the answers.
   2. When you pray, you need to fully give it over to Him!

CHALLENGE/ACTION STEPS

Do you want to stop letting stress/worry control you?

Don't let stress and worry rob you of the peace you could have—focus on God!

Review the Main Points

- Get a proper perspective.
- Put God first in every area of your life.
- Take one day at a time.
- Turn everything over to God.

The Big Idea: Worry and stress take our focus off God and rob us of experiencing true peace in our lives.

All Stressed Out and No Place to Go!

1. What things do you get stressed over?

2. Does worrying help you resolve your problems? What does help you resolve problems?

3. Why do you think we worry so much?

4. What are some positive and negative consequences to worrying?

5. Is there something you are facing right now that makes it difficult for you to trust God? Why is it difficult?

6. How can worry and stress hinder your relationship with God?

7. What worries in your life right now do you need to give over to God?

8. What's one thing that you will put into practice that you heard today?

Overview

Surviving the Storm: The First Water Skier

TOPIC
Surviving the storms in our lives

DESCRIPTION
All of us go through storms. You know—the ones that seem to slap you in the face with a cold, hard wave of water. There are students in your youth ministry who are in the midst of storms. Hopefully this message will be a lifeline you can throw them.

KEY VERSE
"Immediately Jesus reached out his hand and caught him. 'You of little faith,' he said, 'why did you doubt?'" Matthew 14:31

BIBLICAL BASIS
Job 42:1-5; Matthew 14:22-33

THE BIG IDEA
Jesus is in the middle of the storms with us. He's right there, lending us a helping hand and lifting us up when we are down!

PREPARATION
Gather the following props and costumes for the melodrama:
- A bathrobe
- An umbrella
- Four or five squirt guns
- Paper and pens or pencils
- A jar of Grey Poupon mustard

Arrange some chairs in the shape of a "boat" large enough to "hold" the disciples and the Howells.

Outline

Surviving the Storm: The First Water Skier

INTRODUCTION

The Skipper and the Three-Hour Tour

Read the following melodrama (loosely based in Matthew 14:22-33) as an introduction to the message.

Roles

> Jesus, the Skipper
> Peter
> At least two disciples: James and John
> The Howells (a guy and a girl)
> Three waves
> The crowd (everyone else)

Props and Costumes

> A bathrobe (for Jesus to wear)
> An umbrella (for the disciples to carry)
> Four or five squirt guns filled with water (of course) for the "waves"
> Paper and pens for the disciples
> Bottle of Grey Poupon mustard (to be tossed onstage by someone in the audience)
> Chairs arranged in a boat shape

Read the following story, allowing time for the actors to act out their parts:

It was a fine day on the sea of Galilee. Jesus and His disciples had just finished lunch when James let out the loudest burp the disciples had ever heard. The disciples all held up score cards rating James's burp. Jesus gave James one of those looks.

James apologized, "I'm sorry for my uncouth display of bodily functions."

The crowd replied, "That's okay, James!"

Jesus thanked the crowd for their polite gesture.

The disciples owned a tour boat company, taking people on tours of the Sea of Galilee (only during the off-months when they weren't on the Jesus Tour, A.D. 31, that is).

Jesus asked, "Why don't you guys go take the Howells for a three-hour tour? I've got some important things to talk about with the Big Skipper."

So the disciples leaped, skipped and danced their way to their boat. Once inside the boat the disciples shoved off, singing a rousing rendition of the theme song from *Gilligan's Island*. They sang louder. Then they sang even louder.

The crowd gave them a standing ovation for their wonderful rendition. The disciples took a bow.

While in their boat, the waves started getting rough, the tiny ship was tossed—if not for the courage of the fearless crew....The waves crashed into each other. The waves pounded the little boat. The waves crashed over the disciples. They sprayed the boat with water.

The disciples looked around for something to shelter themselves from the waves. They found an umbrella that someone from a previous tour had left on the boat. They opened it up. The waves continued to spray water and crash into each other. Then the waves got tired of this and just decided to lay there.

The disciples and the Howells were scared. They began to quake with fear. They cried. They huddled together in the middle of the boat. Then John remembered something. He began to sing to get their minds off the crashed-out waves. He began to sing "Kumba-ya" *(or another praise song)*. They all joined in. The tune was so catchy that the entire crowd began to sing it.

The storm only got worse. Once again the waves began to beat down on the little boat. The waves sprayed the disciples and the Howells. Even the crowd began to do the wave.

Finally, after a thorough beating, the disciples saw something off in the distance. They all squinted their eyes to see. Was it a bird? Was it a plane? Was it Superman? (Sorry, wrong story!) No, it was Jesus, the Skipper, and He was walking on the waves! Everyone in the boat groaned and shook with fear. They groaned louder. They shook harder.

Finally, Jesus called out to them, "Pardon Me, does anyone have any Grey Poupon?"

Just then, out of the crowd a bottle of the stuff came flying.

"Thanks," Jesus replied.

"You're welcome!" yelled the crowd.

Once again Jesus looked at the disciples cowering in fear, and said, "Hey, don't worry. Be happy! It's me, the Skipper!"

Peter, relieved to see the Skipper, leaped out of the boat and began to walk on the waves. The waves groaned in pain. Peter looked down at the groaning waves. The waves

were tired of being walked on and started to beat on Peter, gently at first, then harder. Peter looked scared, intimidated and pained. He cried out, "Skipper, save me!"

Jesus reached out His hands and the waves calmed, then stopped, then fell to the ground. Jesus reached out and helped Peter back into the tiny boat.

Peter fell on his knees and cried out, "Thank you, Skipper!"

Jesus replied, "It was nothing, little buddy!"

So the day was saved and everyone was relieved, for "if not for the courage of the fearless crew, the Minnow would be lost." The crowd groaned, because it was a lame joke.

The Howells looked at each other and said, "Next year, let's go to Hawaii—by plane!"

Application

Life is filled with storms. Some of you may be in one right now.

- We all will have times when we feel like the disciples did: scared, confused, wondering if we'll ever survive. We wonder where Jesus is in the midst of our storms.
- Some storms are expected, and others just kick the door of your life wide open without warning:
  - Storms of Life: graduation, school, home, family trouble, illness
  - Storms of Doubt: "If God is God, then why can't He…"—screaming for answers to why: divorce, abuse, unanswered prayers, sudden death, etc.
- God seems miles away and way out of reach.

What do you hold on to? What's your anchor in the midst of the storm?

- Christianity isn't just a ticket to heaven—fire insurance—it should impact your life in the here and now!

> **The Big Idea:** Jesus is in the middle of the storms with us. He's right there, lending us a helping hand and lifting us up when we are down!

- He's closer than you've ever dreamed.
- When you can't see Him, He's still there!
- When you can't go on, He'll carry you through those storms.

Read Matthew 14:22-33.

BODY OF THE MESSAGE: A VIEW FROM THE BOAT

I. Jesus Leaves Them in the Storm (Matthew 14:22-24)

A. Jesus allows them to go through the storm.
  1. Jesus knows about the storm and willingly sends the disciples into it.
  2. Verse 23: Jesus goes away to pray—probably for the disciples.
  3. Jesus allows us to go through the storms in our lives.
  4. He knows what's going on in your life today.
B. You can respond by:
  1. *Escaping* the storm (run away from the issue).
  2. *Explaining* the storms (asking God, "Why?").
  3. *Exiting* the storms as soon as possible (*Just get this thing over with*).
  4. *Enduring* the storms with the proper attitude.
C. Our question shouldn't be "Why, God?" but "What are you trying to do in my life?" (i.e., *teaching me, sharpening me, strengthening me, preparing me*, etc.).

II. Jesus Comes to Them in the Storm (Matthew 14:25,26)

A. The storm began early in the evening.
  1. "Where is Jesus when you need Him?" Sound familiar?
  2. "Has He forgotten us?" "Doesn't He care about what's going on?"
B. Jesus finally comes during the fourth watch—3:00 A.M. to 6:00 A.M.
  1. Imagine being between verse 24 and verse 25!
  2. But Jesus *does* come to them in the middle of the storm!
C. Jesus knows about your storms, and He cares. He won't leave you alone in the midst of your storms.

III. Jesus Encourages Them in the Storm (Matthew 14:27)

A. "Take courage." He knows all about the storm.
B. "It is I." Remember who Jesus is, remember what He is capable of doing—miracles: feeding the 5,000, etc.
C. "Don't be afraid." He can do all things and will save even you.

Jesus longs to say the same things to you today. Repeat the three statements.

IV. Jesus Is with Them in the Storm (Matthew 14:28-31)

A. Peter saw Jesus, called to Him and walked on the water toward Him.
  1. Peter sank when he took his focus off Jesus and focused on the storm.

2. He took his focus off the Person above the circumstances and focused on the circumstances. That's when he began to sink!

B. Where is your focus? In the midst of a storm, what do you see—the storm or the Master of the waves?
1. Jesus was only an arm's length away from Peter.
2. Jesus is only an arm's length away from you. Can you see Him?

V. Jesus Is Lord of the Storm (Matthew 14:32,33)

A. Jesus is in control of the storm.
He climbed into the boat and the storm died down.
B. Jesus is the Lord of your storms. He is the One who is in control.
C. He can take a bad situation or circumstance and use it for good.
D. Reach out to Him. He will be your anchor in the midst of the waves and wind of the storm.

CHALLENGE/ACTION STEPS

Seeing God in the Midst of the Storm!

- Jesus is with you in the middle of your storm.
Read Job 42:1-5.

"My ears had heard of you but now my eyes have seen you" (v. 5). After the storm, Job *saw* God instead of only hearing Him!

Review the Main Points

- Jesus knows about the storm.
- When He seems miles away, He's only an arm's length away!
- Focus on Him and reach out to Him. Take courage. Don't be afraid.
- He's right there in the midst of the storm with you!

Prayer

Give students a few minutes to talk with God about their storms, then close.

Surviving the Storm: The First Water Skier

1. What are some of the storms that teenagers face today?

   What are some of the ways teenagers deal with their storms?

2. What are some of the storms in your life right now?

3. How do you deal with the storms in your life?

   How are you dealing with the current storm in your life?

4. How does the fact that Jesus is only an arm's length away impact the storm in your life?

5. What are three action steps you need to implement in your life to deal with your storm?

Overview

Handling the Big T

TOPIC
Handling temptation

DESCRIPTION
All of us go through temptation. Some of us come out victorious; others come out beaten, bruised and defeated. Jesus knows what it's like to be tempted. He faced temptation head on and came out victorious. He was victorious, not only for Himself, but also for us because He left us an example of how to handle the big T. This message is designed to help students realize that Jesus not only understands their temptation, but He was tempted like they are and can help us stand up under any temptation we may face.

KEY VERSE
"For we do not have a high priest who is unable to sympathize with our weaknesses, but we have one who has been tempted in every way, just as we are—yet was without sin." Hebrews 4:15

BIBLICAL BASIS
Psalm 103:11,12; 119:11; Jeremiah 31:34; Matthew 4:1-11; Luke 4:13; 1 Corinthians 10:13; Hebrews 4:14-16; James 1:13-15; 1 John 1:8,9; 2:1,2

THE BIG IDEA
Jesus knows what it's like to be tempted. He understands our temptations and is there to help us resist.

PREPARATION
• Two identical gift boxes
• Tissue paper
• Wrapping paper and ribbon
• A $5 bill
• An envelope
Before the meeting, prepare two identical boxes. Fill one box with paper. Fill the other box with paper and an envelope with $5 in it. Wrap the boxes identically.

Outline

Handling the Big 'T'

INTRODUCTION
Make the following points:

- All of us have faced temptation at some point in our lives. (Give some examples from your own life.)
- Sometimes we come through victorious and sometimes we fall flat on our faces.
- Temptation comes when we are deceived into believing something false—getting something that really isn't there.

The Gift: What You See Isn't Always What You Get!

Ask for two volunteers to come to the front of the room. Have one of the volunteers choose one of the boxes. Give the other box to the other person. Before having them open the boxes, tell everyone that inside one box is $5, while the other box contains nothing. Ask the group members and your volunteers to guess which box contains the $5.

After a few guesses, have the volunteers open the boxes. Ask them the following questions:

1. Why did you think the box that you selected had the $5 in it?
2. What was the only way to find out which box contained the $5?
3. How did you feel when you opened your box and found just paper in it?

Finish the illustration by talking about how temptation is just like the box without the $5. It looks nice on the outside, but when you open it, you'll find out that the promises are just empty. Satan uses empty promises when he tempts us. He promises us fame, popularity or money, but in the end his promises are just as empty as this box.[16]

Temptation comes when we are faced with a situation where we are enticed by what appears on the outside to be something of value to us.

Today, we will look at how Jesus faced temptation and what that means for each of us.

Read Matthew 4:1-11.

BODY OF THE MESSAGE: FOUR HANDLES FOR HANDLING THE BIG *T*

I. Jesus Knew the Tempter

A. Jesus knew all about Satan and how he worked: what his purpose was and what he would do.
   1. Satan would test Him when He was the weakest.
   2. Satan would come and twist the truth/God's promises.
   3. Satan knows where you're the weakest—he knows where/how to tempt you.
   4. Satan is continually about the business of temptation. If he doesn't get you the first time, he'll try again. Luke 4:13 says, "he left him until an opportune time." He'll wait for a better opportunity.

B. Sometimes temptation is blatant, but most often it's subtle, beginning with small issues. When Satan gets you to compromise in small things, he'll drive a wedge between you and God that will make it easier to compromise in increasingly more serious issues.

II. Jesus Knew Temptation

A. Jesus experienced some incredible temptations.
B. He fully played by the rules that God set up in His Word.
C. Jesus could've changed the rules and played by His own set of rules.
D. He went through the temptation with the same rules and power that we have.
E. He experienced the same tough tempting that we do.
   1. Self-centeredness: He could have used His power to meet His own needs (see Matthew 4:3,4).
      Meet MY needs first before anyone else's!
   2. Pride: He could have performed miracles for attention (see vv. 5-7).
      Look at ME and what I can do!
   3. Compromise: He could have compromised His relationship with God (see vv. 8-10).
      No one will ever know—it's just a small thing!
F. Although Jesus was fully human and faced every temptation we do, He was fully God and never gave in to temptation and never sinned.

III. Jesus Knew the Truth

A. Every time Jesus was faced with temptation from Satan, He countered it with the truth in God's Word.
B. Jesus didn't rely on arguing, out-thinking, discussing, etc.
C. Jesus relied on the truth/God's Word—its power and promises.
D. Jesus always focused on God's truth and promises (Psalm 119:11).

IV. Jesus Knows Your Temptation

A. Jesus didn't face temptation so He could get a high five from God; He did it to better understand us and to help us.
B. Hebrews 4:14-16 says Jesus understands what we're going through.
C. First Corinthians 10:13 says He will give us strength and make a way out.

CHALLENGE/ACTION STEPS

1. Know Your Enemy

- Where are you the weakest?
- How are you the most tempted?
- Know that he will return at another opportune time.

2. Know Your God

- Promises—God promises to give you strength and a way out.
- Power—There is power in God's truth and in prayer.
- Plan—Think through your plan of escape from temptation—it will turn temptation into an opportunity to run to God for strength.

Note:
16. For more object lessons, check out *Fresh Ideas Resource 2: Case Studies, Talk Sheets & Discussion Starters* by Jim Burns and Mark Simone (Ventura, Calif.: Gospel Light, 1997), pp. 55-69.

Handling the Big 'T'

1. What are the top 10 temptations teenagers face today?

2. What makes temptation so tempting?

3. What are some of the consequences of giving in to the top 10 temptations?

4. What was a time in your life when you gave in and suffered the consequences of sin?

5. What do the following verses have to say about sin and temptation?

   Psalm 103:11,12

   Psalm 119:11

   Jeremiah 31:34

   1 Corinthians 10:13

   Hebrews 4:14-16

   James 1:13-15

   1 John 1:8,9

   1 John 2:1,2

6. Complete this sentence: "The most difficult area for me in dealing with temptation is..."

7. How does (or should) knowing that Jesus went through temptation help you personally?

8. How can Jesus help you in dealing with temptation?

9. How can your small group members help one another in dealing with temptation?

Overview

Who Do You Listen To?

TOPIC
Self-image, who we are in Christ

DESCRIPTION
Students are bombarded with so many messages every day, telling them what they should be, who they should be like, what they need to have—all to be valued and to appeal to their need for significance. Yet in the midst of all these messages, God's voice seems to get drowned out all too often. This message will challenge students to hear the voice of God: what He thinks about them and how that can impact their everyday life. As you interact during the message, be sure always to point them back to the issue of *How does this affect how I will live my life right now?*

KEY VERSE
"But you are a chosen people, a royal priesthood, a holy nation, a people belonging to God, that you might declare the praises of him who called you out of darkness into his wonderful light." 1 Peter 2:9

BIBLICAL BASIS
Deuteronomy 7:6; Psalm 139:1-17; Romans 8:15; 1 Peter 2:9,10

THE BIG IDEA
In God's eyes you are an original masterpiece, so live like one.

PREPARATION
For Introduction:
- A copy of *It's Not Easy Being a Bunny* by Marilyn Sadler (New York: Beginner Books, A Division of Random House, Inc., 1983)

Familiarize yourself with the story before reading it to students.

For Challenge/Action Steps:
- Small rocks, one for each student

Outline

Who Do You Listen To?

INTRODUCTION

IT'S NOT EASY BEING A BUNNY

This story takes a look at a bunny who decides one day that he doesn't like being a bunny. So he takes off in search of what he really wants to be, only to find out that the best thing he can be is what he was created to be. It's a great story that illustrates the value that God places on each of us, and points out our search for significance.[17]

Read the story to the group and make the following observations:

- We are bombarded with messages every day about what we should be, do, look like, have, etc., to feel valued!
- In the sea of voices, the message that we often lose out on is God's message to us.
- Who do you listen to, when it comes to knowing your value?
- You are important to God (see Psalm 139:17).

Today, I want to challenge you with what God thinks about you!

> **The Big Idea:** In God's eyes you are an original masterpiece, so live like one.

BODY OF THE MESSAGE: FOUR TRUTHS FROM GOD'S LOVE LETTER—1 PETER 2:9,10

I. Truth One: You Are a Chosen People

A. You were hand-selected by God.

B. You are not an accident, but a planned, purposeful creation of God.

C. You were chosen before the world was formed. God knew you and He chose to love you (see Psalm 139:13-16).

D. Despite all that you've been through, no matter where you've been or what you've done, God has chosen to love you!

II. Truth Two: You Are a Royal Priesthood

A. God has given you an incredibly important job to do!

B. You are royal sons and daughters of the King.

C. Old Testament priests were to be God's representatives, to intercede between God and man.

D. You have the incredible job of going before God on behalf of your friends and family.

E. God believes in you so much that He has made you His representative and has given you the job of going before Him on behalf of the people.

III. Truth Three: You Are a Holy Nation

A. You are "set apart"—holy.

B. When you became a Christian, an incredible life change took place.

C. God has called you out of the darkness into His wonderful light.

D. You have a new relationship with God—you can call Him "Daddy" (see Romans 8:15).

E. You have a new relationship with other Christians—a nation/a family/the Body of Christ.

IV. Truth Four: You Are a People Belonging to God

A. Not a possession, but a priceless treasure (see Deuteronomy 7:6).

B. Being a priceless treasure means your owner...
   1. Is willing to pay any price for you.
   2. Has a passion to care for you.
   3. Places great value in you.
   4. Honors you, giving you a special place.

C. You are God's priceless treasure. When you look in the mirror, remember that you are...
   1. Priceless.
   2. Cared for.
   3. Valued.
   4. Honored.

D. God paid the ultimate price for you—Jesus Christ!

CHALLENGE/ACTION STEPS

Review the Four Truths:

You are…
- A chosen people,
- A royal priesthood,
- A holy nation,
- A people belonging to God.

> **The Big Idea:** In God's eyes you are an original masterpiece, so live like one.

How does being valued by God impact your life?
1. Build your life on God's view of you!
2. See who God has made you to be and listen to what He has to say!
3. Live up to your potential—all that God sees in you!

Remembrance Rocks

Hand out small rocks to each student as a visual reminder of the rock-solid fact of what God sees in each of them and believes them to be. The rock is also a reminder to base their lives on the value God holds in them and to live out the reality of that value.

Note:
17. For more storybook ideas, check out *Fresh Ideas Resource 2: Case Studies, Talk Sheets & Discussion Starters* by Jim Burns and Mark Simone (Ventura, Calif.: Gospel Light, 1997), pp. 97-102.

Who Do You Listen To?

1. What are some of the wrong messages that we hear about who we are and who we should be?

2. How do those messages impact how most people live their lives?

3. Which of the four truths affected/challenged/encouraged you the most? How will it change the way you live your life this week?

4. How does it feel to know that you are chosen by God—that He chose you and chose to love you, no matter where you've been or what you've done?

   Is that hard for you to believe? Why or why not?

5. How do you see yourself as a royal priest in your family, school, etc.?

   What can you do to be more of a royal priest in those areas?

6. What are some things that you treasure?

   How are you God's priceless treasure?

   How should knowing that impact the way you live your life?

Bible Study Outlines

Overview

Just Do It!

TOPIC
Applying God's Word

DESCRIPTION
This study examines the issue of applying and living out what students believe to be true. They may believe a lot about God, but are they willing to act on it even when it is costly to them? We only truly believe as much as we live out that belief. The goal is for students to make up their minds to just do it—apply their faith with tangible action.

KEY VERSE
"Do not merely listen to the word, and so deceive yourselves. Do what it says."
James 1:22

BIBLICAL BASIS
Joshua 1:8; Psalm 119:9-11; Romans 15:4; 2 Timothy 3:16,17; Hebrews 4:12; James 1:19-27

THE BIG IDEA
The way we live demonstrates the depth of our faith. God is calling us to put our faith into action.

AIMS OF THIS STUDY
During this study you will guide students to:
- Examine the importance of obedience in the life of the believer;
- Discover what it takes to live out their faith in Jesus Christ;
- Implement a plan of action for applying the Word to their lives.

PREPARATION
- Two pieces of paper for each student
- Several felt-tip pens

Outline

Just Do It!

INTRODUCTION

Agree or Disagree

Give each student two pieces of paper. Have several felt-tip pens available to be passed around the room. Have them write "Agree" in big letters on one piece of paper and "Disagree" on the other piece. Read the following statements. Have each student hold up the sign that expresses his or her opinion. Discuss why they chose their answers.

1. The Bible makes sense to me.

2. I don't get anything out of the Bible.

3. What I read in the Bible doesn't affect my life.

4. The Bible is the source of authority in my life.

5. The level of your beliefs is demonstrated by your actions.

Explain:

> Today, we'll look at what it takes to really live out what we say we believe. We say we believe a lot of stuff about God, but does it really impact how we live? It should!

The Big Idea: The way we live demonstrates the depth of our faith. God is calling us to put our faith into action.

Read James 1:19-27.

IN THE WORD

Three Ingredients for Just Doing It

I. Tackle the Obstacles (see James 1:19-21)

A. One of the first things we need to do to "Just do it!" is to tackle those things that stand in our way.

B. Discuss the following:

1. What are some of the obstacles that stand in the way of living out our faith or applying God's Word?

2. According to James 1:19-21, what are some obstacles listed there?

3. What is the relationship between speaking, listening and anger?

   How can the misuse of these three attributes cause trouble?

4. What is the Christian supposed to get rid of?

   What are some examples you can think of?

5. What does it mean to "humbly accept the word planted in you"?

II. Tangible Application (see James 1:22-25)

A. After we tackle the obstacles in our lives that keep us from living out our faith by applying God's Word, we need to listen to God's Word and apply it!

B. God calls us to do more than just listen to the Word, or even to just read the Word. He calls us to apply it to our lives.

C. Discuss the following:

1. What analogy does James use to describe a person who doesn't apply Scripture?

2. What promise does James give to the person who studies God's Word and applies it?

3. What makes it hard for us to apply/practice what we know we should do?

4. What do you think are some of the benefits of applying God's Word and some consequences for not applying God's Word?

5. What do the following verses have to say about God's Word?

Joshua 1:8

Psalm 119:9-11

2 Timothy 3:16,17

Hebrews 4:12

III. Take Action (see James 1:26,27)
A. The most important part of applying God's Word is taking action on that application. Just do what He says!
B. James challenged Christians to apply their faith in tangible ways.
C. Discuss the following:

1. What are some of the ways James challenges Christians to apply their faith?

2. How do we do those things?

Just Do It!

1. What are some obstacles you need to remove in your life?

   How can we help as a group?

2. What do you need to change this week to have your life match your talk/belief?

CHALLENGE/ACTION STEPS

What action will you take this week to apply God's Word in your life?

Overview

With Help from Little Friends

TOPIC
God will use you if you allow Him to.

DESCRIPTION
In studying the feeding of the 5,000, we become aware that the key ingredient was not the day, the crowd, the messages, the disciples, or even the food. It was the boy who had the lunch bag and the courage to come forward and offer something seemingly insignificant to the Lord. Jesus used the seemingly puny gift of a child's lunch to create one of His most dramatic miracles.

KEY VERSE
"Here is a boy with five small barley loaves and two small fish, but how far will they go among so many?" John 6:9

BIBLICAL BASIS
Micah 6:8; Matthew 14:14,18; Luke 12:27-30; John 6:1-15

THE BIG IDEA
We often hold ourselves back from God's plan because we see ourselves as having nothing of value to offer, but when we give what we have, He can work miracles.

AIMS OF THIS STUDY
In this study you will guide students to:
- Examine the truth that even the gift that seems insignificant or useless can become a miracle in God's hands;
- Discover that God has given them gifts for use in ministry;
- Implement ways to offer back to God the gifts He has given them.

PREPARATION

If you choose to do the optional activity for **Reading the Word,** you might need to gather some simple props and costumes.

- Crackers or cookies (Goldfish crackers would be perfect!)
- A few baskets to hold the "loaves and fishes"
- Simple biblical costumes

Outline

With Help from Little Friends

INTRODUCTION: PYRAMID BUILDING

Ask for 14 volunteers for building a pyramid to illustrate what you are working to accomplish together. Have the first five get in a line on their hands and knees shoulder-to-shoulder, all facing the same direction. The next four fill in the spaces on their backs, the next three do the same, then two, and finally, the top person (see diagram). You'll need other people to help get the volunteers to the higher levels.

The finished pyramid should look like this (each X indicates a person):

```
        X
      X   X
    X   X   X
  X   X   X   X
X   X   X   X   X
```

If needed, you can make a pyramid with 10 volunteers for smaller groups, beginning the first row with four people instead of five.

   With the pyramid still standing, point out what would happen if any person in any row (from the bottom) were suddenly pulled out, or if he or she collapsed. The whole structure would fall apart. From the strongest to the weakest, everyone is needed to create and maintain the structure.

READING THE WORD: "TAKE MY LUNCH!"

Before reading the passage, discuss the following questions. Focus on drawing from students the realization that all of us have lots to offer in doing God's work.

1. What are some of the gifts that make our pastor an effective minister for Christ?

   How about your favorite teacher or coach?

2. Name an adult who has helped you in your Christian growth. How has he or she touched you?

3. Identify an ability that you have that Jesus might be able to use to reach others.

4. How might age limit our effectiveness for Christ?

   Here is an account in God's Word about someone who may have been younger than any of you here and how he presented to Jesus the raw material needed for one of Christ's most dramatic miracles.

   Read John 6:1-15.

Optional: Have your students act out John 6:1-15. Assign or seek volunteers for the parts of:
   Jesus
   the narrator
   Philip
   Andrew
   the boy
   other disciples
   the crowd.
Ask the narrator to allow the actors time to interpret the actions as the passage is being read. The more creative the better. If you wish, set up food props and let the disciples hand out cookies or crackers. You may also want to have costumes for some of the characters. Also, let the actors imagine what the crowd, the boy and the other disciples might have said. This really drives the scene home.

IN THE WORD
After the role play, reread John 6:1-15 and make the following points:

I. Jesus Had Compassion

   A. Read Matthew 14:14—Jesus saw the crowd and had compassion!
   B. Compassion is not just feeling sorry for someone, but really hurting for and with them.
   C. "I know what's going on in your life. I know your needs, and I care!"
   D. Jesus knows each of our needs and cares about each of them.
      1. He sees the needs of those around us as well.
      2. Don't ever think that your needs or others' needs are too big or too small for God to help you.
      3. Read Luke 12:27-30—God knows our needs.

II. Jesus Was the Answer

A. Jesus was the answer for the needs of the crowd.

B. In John 6:7 the disciples were focused on the need and missed the answer—Jesus.

C. Verse 6:8,9: Andrew had an idea—but how far will that go?
Isn't that just like us: "But God, can you really do it? Can you really use *me*?"

D. He *is* powerful enough to meet the needs of others.

III. Bring What You Have to Jesus

A. Matthew 14:18: "Bring them here to me."
1. "Give me what you have and I'll do something with it."
2. Bring your gifts, talents, dreams, etc. to Jesus.
3. Bring what you have and lay it at the feet of Jesus and in His hands. He can do the incredible!

B. How do you bring things to Jesus? By prayer!
1. God is faithful to meet your needs, no matter how big they may seem.
2. What you bring to Jesus can meet your needs and the needs of others.

C. God will use you to meet the needs of others.
The question is, Will you bring your gifts, talents and abilities to God?

With Help from Little Friends

1. What gifts do you possess that God can use?

2. What is required for God to be able to use them?

3. Why do we often try to hide or ignore our gifts?

4. How damaging can false humility or unwillingness be to God's work?

5. Who do you know that have needs in their lives?

    What can you do to help meet those needs?

Overview

Hey, You Got a Call from God!

TOPIC
The Christian's calling from God

DESCRIPTION
Every Christian has a calling from God. It may be a calling to full-time ministry, to an overseas mission field, or to our own neighborhoods—but every believer has a calling! That calling is our ministry: ministering in the lives of those around us, wherever God may place us. This study takes a look at the Christian's calling: how to find and fulfill it!

KEY VERSE
"For I have come down from heaven not to do my will but to do the will of him who sent me." John 6:38

BIBLICAL BASIS
Genesis 12:1-4; Exodus 3:1-10; 1 Samuel 16; Proverbs 16:9; Matthew 4:18-22; Luke 1:26-38; John 6:38; Acts 9:1-19; Ephesians 4:11-13; 1 John 2:5,6

THE BIG IDEA
God is calling every Christian to make an impact on the world.

AIMS OF THIS STUDY
In this study, you will guide students to:
- Examine the five basic principles of God's call upon their lives;
- Discover their own calling in the big picture;
- Implement a lifestyle of living out their calling.

PREPARATION

For Introduction:

- Gather enough blindfolds for half the number of group members.

Set up a simple obstacle course using chairs and other obstacles on hand.

For In the Word:

- Overhead projector, white board or chalkboard, or poster board

Outline

Hey, You Got a Call From God!

INTRODUCTION: TRUST WALK

Have everyone find a partner. Each partner will take turns being the blindfolded person and being the leader. The leader leads the blindfolded partner through an obstacle course (which you set up ahead of time) or unfamiliar outside terrain using *only* verbal commands and warnings.

Have the trust-walk partners form small groups of four to six people with other pairs, then discuss their feelings about the experience by discussing the following:

1. What was it like being the blindfolded player? The leader?

2. How well did you complete the course?

3. What problems did you encounter?

4. On a scale of one to five, with five being high and one being low, describe your level of trust in your leader.

Relate this experience to seeking God's will for the future.

IN THE WORD

I. How and Why We Are Called

In the same small groups, assign one or more of the following passages to each group. Have each group read the assigned passage(s) and answer the following questions about their verses:

Genesis 12:1-4—Abraham	Luke 1:26-38—Mary
Exodus 3:1-10—Moses	Matthew 4:18-22—Disciples
1 Samuel 16—David	Acts 9:1-19—Paul

How were they called?

For what purpose were they called?

- Use as many of the passages as you would like or have time for. Have the groups share their answers with the whole group. Make a list of all the answers for everyone to see on an overhead projector transparency, white board or chalkboard or a piece of poster board.
- Have students return to their small groups and discuss the following question:

  What is the difference between a calling and a career choice (i.e., a call comes from God; a career choice is motivated by self-concerns)?

Have each small group share their responses with the whole group. Following the discussion, share the following five basic principles of how God calls Christians to His purpose for their lives.

II. Five Principles for the Call

A. **God calls in different ways.** For example:
1. Through direct contact as with Moses or the disciples;
2. Through another as with Samuel and David;
3. Through circumstances as with Daniel or Joseph.
B. **God calls for specific tasks and circumstances.**
1. All of these Bible characters were called to fulfill a special place in God's plan.
2. Their significance was often realized "after the fact."
3. In the midst of service, the importance of our task may seem trivial or unimportant but God uses all things for good.
4. Usually in hindsight, we see our value.
C. **God places a common call on all of us** in terms of our character and our service to Him (see Ephesians 4:11-13; 1 Thessalonians 5:24; 1 John 2:5,6).
D. **God has a plan for you to serve Him** in a very specific and direct way in terms of your career, family, community, and church.
E. **The call requires patience.**
1. For many, like Abraham, Joseph, and others including the disciples, God's call was revealed and fulfilled over time after much trial, learning and spiritual growth.
2. Seize the opportunity to be patient before God and to receive His wisdom and guidance.

Hey, You Got a Call From God!

1. What are some of your talents/gifts?

2. If you could do anything for God and know you'd be successful, what would you want to do?

3. How can you give God your dreams, talents and gifts to be used?

4. Is there anything God is calling you to now?

5. On a scale of 1 to 10 with 10 being excellent, how are you doing at being patient with God's calling?

6. Read Proverbs 16:9. Are you allowing the Lord to direct your steps?

Overview

What's Your Problem?

TOPIC
Dealing with conflict

DESCRIPTION
Christians often fear and avoid conflict. Yet the early apostles argued and fought about the essential issues of their day. This study explores some of the disagreements in the Early Church and draws some conclusions about conflict among Christians and how it should be managed.

KEY VERSE
"When the Jewish believers heard this, they stopped arguing." Acts 11:18 (*NCV*)

BIBLICAL BASIS
Acts 10; 11:1-19; 15:1-29; Ephesians 4:26,29

THE BIG IDEA
Conflict is a part of life even among Christians. When facing conflict, the Bible teaches how we should face it, resolve it and get on with the work of God.

AIMS OF THIS STUDY
During this study you will guide students to:
- Examine how conflict is a normal part of human interaction;
- Discover that through conflict we settle our differences and move on;
- Implement a plan for dealing with conflicts when they arise.

Outline

What's Your Problem?

INTRODUCTION

Divide students into smaller groups. Ask each group to develop a skit that illustrates a problem that is common to contemporary teen culture. Suggest things such as gang activity, parent issues, sibling rivalry, school issues, friendship difficulties, etc. Instruct them to go into separate rooms, write a brief (two to three minutes) skit, and rehearse it to be performed before the rest of the groups. The skit should demonstrate a conflict that includes an argument.

The catch is to challenge them to come up with two outcomes for their skit. The first outcome should demonstrate what it might be like without using Christian principles or allowing God to be part of the solution. The second should bring godly principles into the situation. Of course, the second alternative should be the goal.

Give groups a time limit of no more than 15 minutes to put their skits together. Then allow only 15 minutes for all of the groups to perform the skits. Watch your time carefully so that this exercise will not consume the entire meeting without allowing for the Bible study portion.

IN THE WORD

Paraphrase the story of Peter's vision in Acts 10 before looking at Acts 11 and 15. Read the listed Scripture passages, making the following points:

I. The Early Church Faced Serious Issues

A. Read Acts 11:1-3.
B. Conflict had the potential of destroying the unity of the Church.
C. The issues were based on whether or not Jewish believers could associate with Gentiles for the purpose of evangelism.

II. Discussion Brought Understanding and Unity

A. Read Acts 11:4-19.
B. The arguing ceased because they faced their disagreements and talked it through.

III. They Gathered to Talk About the Issues

A. Read Acts 15:1-6.
B. The circumcision issue (whether or not Gentile Christians needed to be circumsized to be saved) causes controversy.
   1. Early Christian missionaries shared Christ, not Jewish custom.
   2. Because of this, disagreements arose.
C. Remember, these were all Christians who were arguing.
D. They gathered to talk it through (see v. 6).

IV. They Referred to Scripture

A. Read Acts 15:12-18.
B. Look at the process of gathering, listening, discussing and drawing some conclusions.
C. Imagine how the discussion proceeded.
   1. Was it ho-hum or passionate with loud voices and arguing and disputes? Play it out for students.
   2. Note Simon's conclusions.

V. They Resolved the Conflict

A. Read Acts 15:19-29.
B. They concluded that Gentiles need not follow Jewish practices to be saved.
   1. They listed the important issues to be followed—those with spiritual ramifications.
   2. They dropped the nonessentials.
   3. They decided to send church leaders to help convey the message face-to-face so that further confusion could be avoided.

CONCLUSION
Things to Note About How the Early Church Dealt with Conflict
- They disagreed.
- They argued.
- They gathered to deal with it.
- They did not leave until it was settled.
- They concluded in agreement.
- They shared the conclusion with others.

Personal Sharing

- Let the students discuss times in their lives when resolution of conflict brought a deeper understanding of an issue.
- Make the point that God does not want believers to avoid conflict to have a peace that will not last. Rather, He desires us to be seek the truth and work out conflicts.

Further Scriptural Help

Often Christians miss the purpose and meaning of anger. Refer to Ephesians 4:26: "'In your anger do not sin': Do not let the sun go down while you are still angry." Explain that anger causes you to underline your convictions, letting others know what you are passionate about, emphasizing why you feel strongly about an issue and perhaps righting a wrong. There is nothing wrong with anger. However, there is one rule: Do not allow your anger to become the cause of sin.

Also refer to Ephesians 4:29: "Do not let any unwholesome talk come out of your mouths, but only what is helpful for building others up." Help students realize that anger should not be expressed in rage and it should not be used to manipulate others. The goal of our conflict is to grow together in Christ.

What's Your Problem?

1. What was the last conflict you had with someone? (Please, give no names!)

   What was it about?

   What, if anything, did you do to resolve the situation?

   If you did not resolve the issue, what needs to be done to resolve it?

2. Think about the person you have the most conflict with. Why do you think you have so much conflict with that person? (Please, give no names!)

3. Finish the sentence "I seem to encounter a lot of conflict when it comes to..."

4. What are some of the ingredients that cause conflict? (Examples: people not listening, gossip, differing opinion, lack of information, etc.)

5. Finish the sentence "I usually handle conflict by..." (Examples: Walking away, shouting, laughing it off, giving in, compromising, getting really mad, pouting, being cruel, getting physically violent, confronting that person.)

6. What is one thing that you learned from this lesson on how to deal with conflict?

Overview

What a Character You Are!

TOPIC
The development of Christian character

DESCRIPTION
This study helps students discover that Christian character is developed by the process in which God uses problems and troubles to "grow us up" in Christ. Experiences and hardships become His tools for our betterment.

KEY VERSES
"We also rejoice in our sufferings, because we know that suffering produces perseverance; perseverance, character; and character, hope. And hope does not disappoint us, because God has poured out his love into our hearts by the Holy Spirit, whom he has given us." Romans 5:3-5

BIBLICAL BASIS
Nehemiah 8:10; Psalm 127:1; Romans 5:3-5; 8:28; Galatians 5:22; James 1:3,4

THE BIG IDEA
Christian character—Christlikeness—is the outcome of our encounters with our life experiences.

AIMS OF THIS STUDY
During this study you will guide students to:
• Examine the development of Christian character;
• Discover how submitting to God's will leads to spiritual maturity;
• Implement a choice to obey God and seek to develop Christian character.

PREPARATION
For Introduction:
• Paper
• Pens or pencils

Outline

What a Character You Are!

OPENING STATEMENT

Begin the lesson by saying something like this:

In my personal life I have had some real messes and problems *(share an example or two)*. Yet, as a Christian, I have discovered that God used these difficult times to provide me with lessons that I could not have learned without them. In other words, in God's hands these experiences were turned into lessons for living.

Someone has said that "life is a house we build as we go along." To the Christian, this house is being built by God for our good (see Psalm 127:1).

Psychologists tell us that character is the person you know (or become) over time. That means that a person's character is something that develops over time. It is not something that he or she simply wakes up one morning and has.

In this lesson we'll look at what God has to do with our character development and what we can count on as a result of that development.

INTRODUCTION: REMEMBER WHEN

Distribute paper and pens or pencils to students. After they are settled, say,

"Remember When" is a memory game that helps us recall our childhoods. Fold your paper in half, like a booklet. On the front print "Remember When" and your name. Number the inside pages 2 and 3, the back as 4.

You'll have five minutes to list on page 2 some of the things you experienced in childhood. Quickly list things you liked, did, thought, believed, were afraid of, watched on TV, vacations you took, pets, anything you remember about your elementary and junior high years.

Give them five minutes to do this, then say:

Now, on page 3 you will mingle with the rest of the group to share and compare your lists. Your goal is to get as many initials as you can of others in the

room who have had any similar experiences. Don't worry about noting the particular thing that you and the other person did that were the same. You're looking for shared occurrences, not specifics. We'll use page 4 later.

Let them gather initials and call them back to their seats in 7 to 10 minutes.

Optional

You may want to make a master sheet prior to the meeting and distribute it to the kids rather than have them each make one. If you do, decorate it with page numbers, the title, a place for their names, and have borders on each page.

IN THE WORD

Read Romans 5:3-5. Discuss with students how God can add meaning to life experiences by using them for our growth and Christian character development. Ask for feedback to the question, "How have you seen this in your life?"

I. Elements of the Process

A. Joy (v. 3)
   1. Joy is the abiding sense that Christ is with us through and in everything.
   2. Joy in the Lord brings strength (see Nehemiah 8:10).

B. Troubles (v. 3)
   1. We all have troubles; they are an inevitable part of life.
   2. They do not define our lives or who we are as people.
   3. They come and go.
   4. Giving them to God has benefits.

C. Patience (v. 3)
   1. Patience is a learned discipline.
   2. It is a fruit of the Spirit (see Galatians 5:22; James 1:3,4).
   3. It is God's tool to make the troubles we face have meaning.

D. Character (v. 4)
   1. The process of becoming like Jesus.
   2. Character is what defines us as Christians.
   3. It is character that allows Christ to shine through us.
   4. It is in our Christian character that the Holy Spirit takes hold of our lives and transforms us to be like Jesus.

   E. Hope (v. 4)
       1. In hope we look ahead beyond what we face to what we are becoming.
       2. In hope we see past today's troubles and see God in front of us, clearing the path.
       3. Hope is the knowledge for today that tomorrow will be different.
   F. God's Presence (v. 5)
       1. God assures us that He is with us in these difficult and troubling times.
       2. The process leads us into a closer understanding of God and how God can convert the junk of our lives into beautiful works of art.
       3. You are that work of art!

II. The Outcome of the Process

   A. As we endure the troubles and allow the lessons to be taught, we gain an inner sense and knowledge that God is with us through our problems.
   B. We are not alone in the struggles—God is there.
   C. We are not helpless—God stands with us.

III. A Time for Personal Sharing

It is guaranteed that students will have much to say about this topic. Channel the discussion into sharing about how they see God's hand in their lives in the midst of trouble. This sharing is important to help them understand problems in a new way. They begin to see that hardship is not random or senseless, but that, when turned over to God, difficulty is a tool the Holy Spirit uses to form us into Christlikeness.

What a Character You Are!

1. Why is it sometimes hard to feel God's presence in the middle of trouble?

2. Who are some Bible characters who grew stronger, or wiser, etc., from troubles they encountered?

3. What can we do to become more aware of God's guiding hand in our lives?

4. What should the goal or outcome of our lives be?

5. Where would we be without God's instruction and training?

6. Have any of you ever resisted God's leading in a time of trouble? Tell us about that.

"REMEMBER WHEN" REVISITED

Now turn to page 4 in your "Remember When" booklets. For the next few minutes, think about how you can see Jesus' character developing in your life. Be honest with yourself. This is not the time to humbly say that there is no evidence. Remember that we honor God by letting Him have a place in our lives. This is a moment to acknowledge that place you have given Him. List some of the good works that speak of your developing Christian character. Consider changed attitudes or new priorities, mission trip or work camp experiences, special church services you have helped with, etc.

Keep this paper in your Bible and refer to it often as you continue your walk with Christ. You'll experience times of pain, trouble and hardship throughout your life. Add to the list as you see God continuing to work in your life, developing Christlike character. Let this list be a reminder that there is a reason for difficult times.

Remember, in Christ you'll become a *real* character!

Overview

Becoming a Great Christian

TOPIC
The Great Commission

DESCRIPTION
This study explores the Great Commission given by Jesus to His followers. The goal is for each Christian in the group to feel a personal call to live a lifestyle of personal commitment to fulfill the Great Commission, wherever God takes them in life.

KEY VERSE
"Therefore go and make disciples of all nations, baptizing them in the name of the Father and of the Son and of the Holy Spirit, and teaching them to obey everything I have commanded you. And surely I am with you always, to the very end of the age." Matthew 28:19,20

BIBLICAL BASIS
Matthew 9:37; 28:16-20; Acts 1:8

THE BIG IDEA
As Christians, we are called to carry out the Great Commission, making disciples and carrying on the faith.

AIMS OF THIS STUDY
During this study you will guide students to:
- Examine what Jesus commanded in the Great Commission;
- Discover how the Great Commission relates to every believer;
- Implement a lifestyle of ministry by accepting the Great Commission as a personal call for each of their lives.

Outline

Becoming a Great Christian

INTRODUCTION: THE GREAT FISH CONTROVERSY

Read the following story and discuss the questions:

For months, the Fishermen's Society had been wracked with dissension. They had built a new meeting hall which they called Aquarium Hall and had even called a world-renowned Fisherman's Manual scholar to lecture on the art of fishing. But still no fish were caught.

Several times each week they would gather together in their ornate Aquarium Hall, recite portions of the Fisherman's Manual and listen to the scholar expose the intricacies and mysteries of the manual. The meeting would usually end with the scholar dramatically casting his net into the large tank in the center of the hall and the members rushing excitedly to its edges to see if any fish would bite. None ever did, of course, since there were no fish in the tank, which brings up the reason for the controversy.

The temperature of the tank was carefully regulated to be just right for ocean perch. Indeed, oceanography experts had been consulted to make the environment of the tank nearly indistinguishable from the ocean. But still no fish. Some blamed it on poor attendance at the Society's meetings. Others were convinced that specialization was the answer. Perhaps several smaller tanks geared especially for different fish groups would work. There was even a division over which was more important: casting or providing optimum tank conditions. Eventually a solution was reached.

A few members of the Society were commissioned to become professional fishermen and were sent to live a few blocks away on the edge of the sea and do nothing but catch fish. It was a lonely existence because most other members of the Society were terrified of the ocean. So the professionals would send back pictures of themselves holding their catches and letters describing the joys and difficulties of real, live fishing. And periodically they would return to Aquarium Hall to show slides. After such meetings, people of the Society would return to their homes thankful that their Hall had not been built in vain.

1. What's the main point of this story?

2. What can we do to keep this story from being the story of our lives?

IN THE WORD
Read Matthew 9:37.

I. Make Me an Instrument

Francis of Assisi was a wealthy, highborn man who lived hundreds of years ago. He felt that his life was incomplete, and even though he had more than enough wealth, he was an unhappy man. One day, while he was riding, he met a leper. The leper was ugly and repulsive because of the decay of his disease. Something moved Francis to dismount and fling his arms around this person. In the arms of Francis, the leper's face changed into the face of Christ. Francis was never the same again.

Francis of Assisi spent the rest of his life serving his Lord Jesus Christ. He wrote the following words as a prayer to God from the heart of a man who had a deep desire to be an instrument of God's will on this earth:

> Lord, make me an instrument of Your peace.
> Where there is hatred, let me sow love;
> Where there is injury, pardon;
> Where there is doubt, faith;
> Where there is despair, hope;
> Where there is darkness, light;
> And where there is sadness, joy.

Consider Francis's poem and then read Matthew 9:37. What does Jesus mean when He says, "The harvest is plentiful but the workers are few"?

Why is Francis of Assisi's prayer so important for living a lifestyle of ministry?

Read Matthew 28:16-20. How does Francis's prayer fit into the Great Commission?

II. The Great Commission

    A. Jesus' Authority (see v. 18)
        1. Jesus' authority came from His heavenly Father.
        2. Jesus was sending His disciples out on the basis of that authority.
    B. Jesus' Command (see v. 19)
        1. "Go"—takes effort and initiative to reach out to others.
        2. "Make disciples"—evangelize, adding new believers.
        3. "Baptizing"—helping those followers identify with Jesus, publicly proclaim their decision.
        4. "Teaching"—helping people grow in their faith and relationship with Jesus Christ.
    C. Jesus' Promise (see v. 20)
        1. Jesus promised them that He would be with them.
        2. Jesus promised them His help in the process.
        3. He promised to be with them in the process of what He commanded them to be about—reaching out to others, living a lifestyle of ministry.

Before beginning the discussion, tell students the following:

The most influential people in our lives don't have to be famous or have it "all together." They are just people who love God, seek Him, and take the initiative in reaching out to others. You can be influential in others' lives.

Becoming a Great Christian

1. Who are the five most influential people in your life and why are they influential?

2. What fears do people have when it comes to telling others about Jesus Christ?

3. How do you think the disciples felt after hearing Jesus' promise (Matthew 28:20)?

   How do you feel?

4. When Jesus ascended into heaven, He entrusted the job of making disciples to people like you and me (see Acts 1:8). How does that make you feel? How does that challenge you personally?

5. What makes this Great Commission such an important task?

6. What challenges does the Great Commission give you personally?

CHALLENGE/ACTION STEPS

Who in your life right now needs your love, care and witness of Jesus Christ? List three people.

What can you do to begin to fulfill the Great Commission during this next week?

What can we do as a group?

Overview

Now You See Him; Now You Don't

TOPIC
Faith

DESCRIPTION
Faith and doubt are some of the biggest issues that students face: *What is faith? Why do I sometimes feel like I doubt God all the time?* This study addresses the issue of faith and where our faith should be placed.

KEY VERSE
"Now faith is being sure of what we hope for and certain of what we do not see." Hebrews 11:1

BIBLICAL BASIS
John 20:19-31; Hebrews 11:1; Revelation 2:10

THE BIG IDEA
You must have faith to believe in a God who you cannot see.

AIMS OF THIS STUDY
In this study you will guide students to:
• Examine how God's Word defines "faith";
• Discover how faith impacts our relationship with Christ;
• Implement a choice to live out faith in areas of doubt.

PREPARATION
For the Warm-Up:
• An apple, a lemon, an orange, and a pear (or similar fruits)
• Four paper plates, one for each type of fruit
Cut the apple, lemon, orange and pear into several slices before the lesson and place them on the paper plates.

For Challenge/Action Steps:

- 3x5-inch index cards and pens or pencils, enough for each student to have one of each

Outline

Now You See Him; Now You Don't

INTRODUCTION: SO WHAT DO YOU THINK?

Divide the room down the middle. The left side of the room will be the agree side and the right side of the room will be the disagree side. Have the students stand up and move to the appropriate side of the room based on if they agree or disagree with the following statements. Interact with a few of the students on the agree side and the disagree side as you discuss each statement:

1. Believing in things I can't see is easy.

2. Faith is for those who need something to believe in because they can't deal with reality.

3. Faith is believing in something only when you know it's true.

4. Jesus' disciples were always men of faith.

5. If a Christian doesn't always have faith, something's wrong with him or her.

6. Believing in Jesus is sometimes difficult because I can't see Him.

7. I can believe in God without having any faith.

WARM-UP: FAITHFUL FRUIT

Have the students return to their seats and read or say the following:

In every part of our lives, we are required to believe in things that we don't see. At school we have faith that our learning will someday help us. When we get in a car, we have faith that it will start. When we turn on the water faucet, we

have faith that the water will pour out. In fact, most things we do require some faith. Let's see how faith works.

The following exercise is designed to demonstrate how faith works. Select four students and send them outside the room. Call each student back into the room one at a time. Have sample pieces of fruit hidden from the student. Have the student put on a blindfold. Give the student one piece at a time of each of the fruits. Before the student eats the fruit, say the following:

You will now eat a piece of _____.

The trick is to feed the student the lemon when saying "orange" the first time. The second time you say "orange," see what he or she does, but make sure he or she gets the orange the second time. Be truthful when you name the rest of the fruits before asking each student to taste the fruit. After you have fed each student the four pieces of fruit, have him or her remove the blindfold. When all four have tasted the fruit, discuss the following questions:

1. How did you feel eating something you couldn't see? Did you believe it was what I said it was going to be before you ate it?

2. How did you feel when you tasted a lemon when I told you that you were going to receive an orange?

3. What did you think you were going to get when I again told you that you were going to receive an orange?

4. Did it take faith for you to eat what you were given without seeing it?

IN THE WORD
Read Hebrews 11:1 and discuss the following questions:

1. Did you agree or disagree with the statement, "Faith is believing in something only when you know it's true"?

2. How would you explain what "being sure of what we hope for" means?

3. How would you explain what "certain of what we do not see" means?

4. Does faith then require us to believe in something that we can't see?

5. Since we can't see God, does it take faith to believe in Him? Why?

After discussing the Hebrews passage on what faith is, have the students divide into small groups of four to six members. They will discuss the story of doubting Thomas in John 20:19-31.
   Begin the small-group time by saying,

> There are many of us who don't always have faith. In fact, all of us at various times in our lives will have doubt. Even one of Jesus' disciples doubted that Jesus was raised from the dead. Read John 20:19-31 about doubting Thomas and then discuss the questions together.

1. Was Thomas sure of things hoped for and certain of things not seen? Did Thomas have faith? Explain your answer.

2. How have you felt like Thomas in the last week?

3. Is believing in things that you cannot see easy? Explain.

4. How does verse 29 relate to Hebrews 11:1?

CHALLENGE/ACTION STEPS
State the following:

> Now that we know that God is with us even though we can't see Him, and we know that He helps us even though we can't see Him, let's make a decision to leave doubt behind and start trusting Him completely with our whole lives.

   Give a 3x5-inch card and a pen or a pencil to each student. On the 3x5 card have the students write down one area in their lives where it's tough to trust—to have faith in God. Give the students an example from your own life.
   After everyone has written their answers, have them write God's promise in Revelation 2:10—"'Be faithful, even to the point of death, and I will give you the crown of life'"—or Hebrews 11:1—"Now faith is being sure of what we hope for and certain of what we do not see"—on the other side of their cards. Instruct students to place this card in their

wallet, purse, notebook or backpack; and whenever they start to worry, doubt, or lose faith in the area they indicated on their cards, to read the card to remember that they've given the problem over to Him and He will indeed be faithful.

Conclude the time together by praying for each other that God would continue to be evident in their lives and that they would be able to believe and have faith while in a world that seems to have none.

Overview

You're Not Like Me!

TOPIC
Racism, prejudice and favoritism

DESCRIPTION
Racism, prejudice and favoritism are evils that are alive and well today. Sadly enough, they are just as prevalent and devisive in the Church as they are in the world. This study takes this issue head-on to see what God's Word has to say about racism, prejudice and favoritism. Our desire is that students would be able to walk away with a new appreciation for others who are not like them, whether it be in race, social status, wealth, or any other aspect.

KEY VERSE
"If you really keep the royal law found in the Scripture, 'Love your neighbor as yourself,' you are doing right. But if you show favoritism, you sin and are convicted by the law as lawbreakers." James 2:8,9

BIBLICAL BASIS
Matthew 7:1-6; James 2:1-13

THE BIG IDEA
In Jesus Christ, we are all one, regardless of race, wealth or status.

AIMS OF THIS STUDY
During this study you will guide students to:
- Examine what the Bible has to say about the issue of favoritism;
- Discover the ways in which we show favoritism today;
- Implement a choice to live a lifestyle of equality, unity and love.

PREPARATION
For Introduction Option One:
- A video of *School Ties* (Paramount Pictures, 1993)
- A VCR and TV

Before the meeting, cue the video to the clip of the confrontation when the main character's roommate discovers that he is trying to hide the fact that he is Jewish.

For Introduction Option Two:

- Video camera and blank cassette
- A VCR and TV

Before your meeting, ask selected students some of the questions in Introduction Option One and record their answers on video. Prepare to play the video at the beginning of the study.

Outline

You're Not Like Me!

INTRODUCTION

Option One: *School Ties* Video Clip

In this movie, the main character enters a prestigious prep school and encounters more than just academic challenges. Being Jewish, he discovers the cruelty of racism. The movie chronicles his struggle with who he is, what he wants to be and how others see him. Introduce the video clip, explaining that it is about the confrontation that occurs when the main character's roommate discovers that he is trying to hide the fact that he is Jewish. It's an excellent portrayal of racism, acceptance and being who God created you to be.[1]

After viewing the video segment, ask the following questions:

1. When was a time you felt like an outcast?

2. How would you define the words "racism" and "prejudice"?

3. What do you think are the most damaging things about racism?

4. What do you think God thinks about the issue of racism?

   What are some passages of Scripture that speak about racism?

5. If you could do something to solve the issue of racism, what would you do?

Option Two: Video Interviews

Show the video you filmed ahead of time in which you interviewed students using the questions in Option One above to introduce the topic of racism.

IN THE WORD

Read James 2:1-13.

I. Prejudice Is a Form of Judging (James 2:2-4).

A. When we show favoritism we are really judging that person as better or worse than we are.

B. Favoritism or racism is the result of prejudging others.

What example did James give of someone showing favoritism?

What would be some examples of favoritism, prejudice or racism in our world?

What does Matthew 7:1-6 have to say about judging others?

How do we usually judge others?

II. Prejudice Insults God's Creation (James 2:5-7)

A. When we show prejudice we insult God by belittling what He has created.

B. God has created each of us as different and unique creations. When we show favoritism or prejudice, we are saying that God made a mistake or that everyone needs to be like us.

How does God feel about prejudice?

Why do we often treat some people better than we do others?

How do we tend to show favoritism toward people based on physical appearance, athletic ability, job status or possessions?

III. God Calls Us to Love Others Regardless (James 2:8-11)

A. One of the hardest things to do in the world is to love others who are not like us.

B. Often we attach conditions to our love of others.

What law is found in verse 8? What does it mean to love others as yourself?

What conditions do we attach to others before we will love them?

What does it mean to love others regardless?

What are some practical ways in which we can love others who are not like us?

IV. God Calls Us to Be People of Mercy (James 2:12,13)

A. God calls us to be people of mercy—people who are not partial, showing love to all we come in contact with.

Why is it tough to show mercy to others?

Why should we be merciful?

How can we show mercy in practical ways to others regardless of who they are?[2]

1. For additional video ideas see *Fresh Ideas Resource 2: Case Studies, Talk Sheets and Discussion Starters* (Ventura, Calif.: Gospel Light, 1997), pp. 103-114.
2. For other ideas on how to address racism see *The Year-Round Church Event Book*, "Martin Luther King, Jr. Day" (Ventura, Calif.: Gospel Light, 1998), pp. 52-56.

You're Not Like Me!

1. Why is it wrong to show favoritism to others?

2. How has this study changed the way you look at others?

CHALLENGE/ACTIONS STEPS

What can you do this week to:

- Stop judging?

- Celebrate God's unique creation in others?

- Show love regardless?

- Be a person of mercy?

Who is someone that you have been prejudiced against? When and how will you ask for forgiveness?

Overview

No Fear!

TOPIC
Facing our fears with courage

DESCRIPTION
Trials and difficult situations are a fact of life. Often we find ourselves face-to-face with giants—problems that seem overwhelming to us. These could be problems at home, with relationships, or other difficult circumstances. Can we ever win? This study examines the story of David and Goliath, what it took for David to defeat Goliath, and how to apply those principles to our own lives. No Fear! No Problem!

KEY VERSE
"Saul replied, 'You are not able to go out against this Philistine and fight him; you are only a boy, and he has been a fighting man from his youth.' But David said to Saul,….'The LORD who delivered me from the paw of the lion and the paw of the bear will deliver me from the hand of this Philistine.'" 1 Samuel 17:33,34,37

BIBLICAL BASIS
Joshua 1:9; 1 Samuel 17; Psalm 56:3,4; Matthew 6:25-32; Romans 8:31,32,37-39; 1 John 5:4,5

THE BIG IDEA
No matter how big your enemies, you can face your fear with courage with God on your side!

AIMS OF THIS STUDY
In this study, you will guide students to:
* Examine the story of David and Goliath;
* Discover why David was able to defeat Goliath and how we can overcome the Goliaths in our lives;
* Implement a plan for defeating the giants in our lives.

PREPARATION

For Introduction:
- A deck of cards, or a prepackaged card trick
- A card-trick book

Practice the trick before the meeting.

For In the Word:
- Three pieces of poster board
- Several felt-tip pens

Write one of each of the following questions on a separate piece of poster board:

What are some of the Goliaths in life?
What are some of the Goliaths in the lives of your friends?
What are some of the Goliaths in your life?

For Challenge/Action Steps:
- Note paper
- Envelopes
- Pens or pencils

Outline

No Fear!

INTRODUCTION: HOW DO THEY DO THAT?

Introduce the lesson by doing the card trick. Do the trick a couple of times, or another trick, if time permits.

Explain to your group that what seem to be insurmountable odds can be overcome. What looks impossible could actually happen! Discuss the following:

Have you ever had a situation in your life that seemed to be impossible to overcome? What was it and what happened?

After a few minutes of discussion, say:

Today, we're going to look at David as he faced what seemed to be an impossible situation. Let's check out what he faced, what he did, and what happened.

IN THE WORD

Read 1 Samuel 17.

David faced Goliath and it seemed like he was up against an impossible situation. What Goliath didn't understand was that God was on David's side. With God's help, David was victorious. God is the God of the impossible. He specializes in making impossible situations possible!

Who's Your Goliath?

Tape the three pieces of poster board on the wall. Set out the felt-tip pens. Ask the students to write their answers to the following questions on the poster boards:

What are some of the Goliaths in life?

What are some of the Goliaths in the lives of your friends?

What are some of the Goliaths in your life?

Read several of their answers, then discuss the following:

Have you ever been in a situation that seemed too big for you?

When was a time that you faced a trial or problem that seemed impossible, yet you were victorious in solving that trial or problem?

If you were David, what would be going through your mind during the situation in chapter 17?

David defeated Goliath by hurling a stone at the giant. Let's look at a few stones we can use to slay the giants in our lives.

I. Stone One: Attitude (1 Samuel 17:32-37)

David didn't focus on the size of the giant, but on the size of his God!

What are you focusing on: the size of the problem or the size of your God?

Why is it easier to focus on the trial/problem rather than on God?

How can our attitude help or hinder us in fighting our giants?

What is your attitude mostly like in facing tough situations?

II. Stone Two: Faith (1 Samuel 17:45-47)

A. David had faith in his God. He knew who was in charge!
B. David knew that the God he put his faith in knew his heart.
C. David trusted in God's strength, not in his own or man's strength (vv. 45-47).

What are you relying on to win your battle with your giant?

How does faith help us in fighting the giants of tough times?

How does going through tough times help strengthen our faith?

III. Stone Three: Action (1 Samuel 17:48,49)

A. David didn't wait for Goliath to come to him. He faced the giant (see vv. 48,49).
B. David had a plan to defeat the giant.
C. David wasn't afraid to go after the giant because he knew that the Lord was on his side.

What is your plan of attack for facing the giants in your life?

What things keep us from taking action in tough times?

D. God is big enough to defeat any giant that may come into your life. You can stand up and defeat any problem—no matter how big—when you are on God's side. The battle belongs to God and He will fight for you!

Assign the following verses to different students. Have them read the verses aloud, then discuss how each passage applies to defeating the giants in our lives:

Joshua 1:9
Psalm 56:3,4
Matthew 6:25-32
Romans 8:31,32
Romans 8:37-39
1 John 5:4,5

No Fear!

1. What are some of the giants in your life right now (those things that seem too big to overcome, things over which you need victory)?

2. What are three things that you can do this week to defeat the giants in your life?

3. What is one verse that challenged you, comforted you or spoke to you?

CHALLENGE/ACTION STEPS

In conclusion, you will be given note paper, an envelope and a pen or pencil. Write a letter to God, expressing how you feel and what you have learned from the lesson. You can either write the letter to God, or you can write the letter as though God is writing to you.

   When you have finished, put the letter in the envelope, address it to yourself and return it to your leader. The letters will be mailed to you in a few weeks or a month.

Overview

Forgive? Forget It!

TOPIC
Forgiving others

DESCRIPTION
Forgiveness—all of us want it, but not all of us are willing to freely give it to others. God calls us to forgive others to the same extent that He has forgiven us. It's a high calling, but one that God requires from us. This study explores what it means to truly forgive one another.

KEY VERSE
"Be kind and compassionate to one another, forgiving each other, just as in Christ God forgave you." Ephesians 4:32

BIBLICAL BASIS
Matthew 6:14,15; 18:21-35; Luke 23:32-34; Ephesians 4:32; Colossians 3:13

THE BIG IDEA
We have been forgiven such an incredible amount that God calls us to forgive others to the same extent.

AIMS OF THIS STUDY
In this study, you will guide students to:
• Examine the importance of forgiving others as a part of the Christian life;
• Discover the personal impact that the lack of forgiveness can have on the Christian;
• Implement a choice and a plan for how to be a person of forgiveness.

Outline

Forgive? Forget It!

INTRODUCTION: TALK AROUND

Divide students into groups of no more than four in each group.

Ask each person to share with his or her small group for 20 seconds on the following statements. If your students are shy, start with some easy and fun statements to talk about first. Give a signal when each 20-second interval is up.

Talk about one of the worst things someone has ever done to you.

Talk about a time when you held a grudge against someone.

Explain:

From time to time, all of us get hurt by other people. If there is someone who has hurt you recently, you need to think about forgiving them. Let's look into how forgiving others is an important part of living the Christian life.

A Spontaneous Drama: The Unforgiving Servant

The following is a modified reenactment of Matthew 18:21-35.

Ask for 15 volunteers to act out the following story as you read it. Be sure to allow time for the actors to interpret their actions.

The king	The servant's two kids
The servant	The servant's dog
The throne	A fellow servant
Guard 1	A police officer
Guard 2	Two mysterious men
The servant's wife	
The jail (two people, facing each other and holding hands)	

Jesus told His followers the following story about forgiveness:

God's kingdom works like a certain king who sat down on his throne and said to his guards, "Hey, too many of my servants owe me money! Boys, it's time we collect some cash!"

The guards who stood before the king shouted in unison, "Yes, sire. Whatever you say, sire!"

Then the king said to his guards, "Arrange to have the police go out and find one of my servants who owes me some big bucks and bring him before me!"

The guards replied, "Yes, sire. Whatever you say, sire!" Then they cried out in high-pitched voices: "Police! Police! Help! Police!"

A police officer showed up immediately. The guards whispered to the police officer, telling him the situation, and sent him away to do what the king had commanded.

It didn't take long before the police officer returned with the servant, bringing him right up to the throne. The servant's wife, kids and dog followed behind, whimpering as they came.

Now, it was the custom in the land that whenever people came before the king, the guards would always sing, "The king, the king, the king! You now stand before the king." After this, everyone, even the dog, bowed down to the king.

"Arise, my subjects!" shouted the king. And everyone, even the dog, got back up on their feet.

"Oh, your royal kingliness," said the first guard.

The second guard continued, "This scumbucket of a servant owes you big-time."

"How much?" demanded the king.

The first guard said to the king, "This sewer-sipping servant owes you $100,000."

The king was aghast so he gasped.

The king got off of his throne and walked over to the servant. Then he walked over to the servant's family. He stooped down to pet the dog. The dog licked the king's hand.

The dog said, "Yeeeew."

The king walked over to the servant again and said, "Can you pay me what you owe me?"

The servant stammered and said, "N-n-n-n-n-n-no s-s-s-s-s-s-sir."

The king walked back to the dog and reached down to pet it again. The dog just growled this time. Then the king said, "Away with all of them. Throw my servant in jail and have his family and this mutt sold at auction so I can get some of my money back."

The family cried out together, "Oh no!"

The dog barked and howled.

The guards shouted, "Yes, sire! Whatever you say, sire!"

Just then the servant got down on his hands and knees and crawled over to the king. He tugged at the king's royal robes.

"Your royal royalness," blurted the servant. Then the servant began weeping like a baby. When the crying was over, the servant said, "Please sire, give me another chance and I'll pay you back—every cent!"

The king was touched and said, "I am touched by your plea." The king went on to say, "I am canceling your debt. Take your family home and have some hot cocoa and marshmallows. I'm sure you'll feel better in the morning."

"Oh boy!" shouted the family together. The dog barked. The whole family joyously skipped off toward home.

Later on that very day, while on the road home with his family and dog, the forgiven servant saw a fellow servant who had borrowed five bucks from him the week before. The forgiven servant did not notice that two mysterious men were mysteriously following his family.

He stopped the fellow servant, threw him to the ground and yelled at him. "You deadbeat! Pay me my five bucks right now!"

The fellow servant got to his knees and bowed before him and begged, "Please Barney, give me a chance and I'll pay you back. I've got the money at home, but I just don't have it on me right now."

The servant yelled, "Too bad, Fred. You're going to jail." Then he yelled in a high voice "Police! Police! Help! Police!"

The police officer showed up immediately.

The servant said to the officer, "Take this man away and throw the book at him. He owes me money and he hasn't repaid his debt."

The police officer replied, "What book?"

Then the officer took the fellow servant and threw him in jail.

When the two mysterious men who were lurking mysteriously saw what took place, they shouted out together, "We need to tell the king!" Then they turned around and ran back to see the king.

Well, to make the story shorter, we'll skip the part about how the two mysterious men stopped for lunch, what they had to eat and who they talked with. Anyway, after lunch they came before the king who was sitting on his throne.

The guards sang, "The king, the king, the king! You now stand before the king." Once again, everyone bowed down to the king.

Once again, the king shouted, "Arise, my subjects!" which the two mysterious men did immediately.

Then the first guard said to the king, "Sire, these two mysterious men wish to tell you something."

The two mysterious men approached the king and whispered the whole story to him.

When they finished telling the king what they had seen, the king was really mad. He said, "I am really mad now. Have the police bring in this sin-serving servant."

And the guards shouted, "Yes, sire! Whatever you say, sire!"

The police officer brought the servant in before the king. The guards started singing, "The king, the king, the king! You now stand be...."

But before they could finish, the king yelled, "Guards, enough with that tune already!"

The guards replied, "Yes, sire! Whatever you say, sire!"

"Enough! Enough!" yelled the king. Then the king got up from his throne and walked up to the servant.

Enraged, the king yelled at the servant, "Bad servant! Bad! Bad! Bad! You are evil! I forgave you when you asked for mercy. But you won't forgive your fellow servant who asked for mercy! That really stinks, right, guards?"

The guards shouted, "Yes, sire! Whatever you say, sire!" The king turned to the police officer. "Officer, release the other servant and throw this man into the jail!"

So, that's just what the officer did—he released the other servant and threw the unforgiving servant into the jail and slammed the door behind him. The servant was kept there until he could pay his entire debt—which is a hard thing to do when you are in jail, earning no money.

Jesus ended the story by saying, "This is how my heavenly Father will treat each of you unless you forgive your brother from your heart."

1. After hearing this story, what's your first impression about the king and the servant?

2. Jesus said that this story represents the way things are in His kingdom. So, what do the following story elements represent?

   The king

   The servant

   The $100,000 that the servant owed

   The fellow servant

   The $5 that the fellow servant owed

3. What was Jesus trying to teach His followers in this story?

IN THE WORD
Have students return to their small groups. Then explain:

The Bible has a lot to say about the importance of forgiving others, such as what kinds of wrongs we should forgive, how often we should forgive and why we should forgive. In your group, read the following Scripture verses and answer the questions.

Matthew 6:14,15

What happens to us if we don't forgive others when they sin against us?

Matthew 18:21,22

How often are we supposed to forgive others?

What do you think Jesus was trying to tell His followers by giving them a number of times they should forgive another person?

Colossians 3:13

What kinds of offenses are we supposed to forgive others for?

According to this verse, why should we forgive others?

Luke 23:32-34

Jesus is our example for all things. What was His attitude to those who were killing Him?

How difficult would it be for you to forgive someone who was about to murder you? Explain.

What would have to change in your life to be the kind of forgiving person that Jesus is?

There seems to be a difficulty in comparing Matthew 6:14,15 and Colossians 3:13. The Matthew passage appears to say that we are forgiven by God when we forgive others while the Colossians verse says that we are to forgive others because we have been forgiven by God. How do these two Scriptures fit together?

© 1998 by Gospel Light. Permission to photocopy granted. *Bible Study Outlines and Messages*

- 204 -

Forgive? Forget It!

1. How do we forgive others?

2. What does it look like in a relationship to forgive another person?

3. Who in your life needs to be forgiven?

4. Why is it tough to forgive them? What's been keeping you from forgiving them?

5. What will you do about it this week?

CHALLENGE/ACTION STEPS

We've learned today that forgiving for the Christian is not an option, but a command of God. Even though we may feel hurt and angry at others who have wronged us, we need to forgive others because we have personally been forgiven by God for all of our sins.

   Close in prayer, committing to God your attempts to demonstrate forgiveness during the coming week.

Overview

So You Want to Be a Wise Guy!

TOPIC
Worldly wisdom vs. godly wisdom

DESCRIPTION
We live in a world that is at war with the things of God. All you need to do is turn on the TV and you can see a world that belittles the things of God and elevates worldly wisdom. As Christians, we have a different set of standards and values than the world. The world wants to squeeze us into the mold of its standards and values. This study defines two types of wisdom and their respective outcomes.

KEY VERSE
"But the wisdom that comes from heaven is first of all pure; then peace loving, considerate, submissive, full of mercy and good fruit, impartial and sincere." James 3:17

BIBLICAL BASIS
James 3:13-18

THE BIG IDEA
Being a Christian means living by God's standards and values rather than the world's.

AIMS OF THIS STUDY
During this study you will guide students to:
- Examine two different types of wisdom and values;
- Discover the outcome of both types of wisdom;
- Implement a choice to live by God's wisdom, rather than the world's.

PREPARATION
Purchase or borrow a Jenga game. Set up the game on a sturdy, flat surface.

Outline

So You Want to Be a Wise Guy!

INTRODUCTION: WHAT'S YOUR FOUNDATION?

Here's a great way to visually illustrate the foundation on which we build our lives. Before the meeting begins, set up the Jenga game block tower on a flat surface.

Begin by asking the group:

"What is it that people try to build their lives on?"

Allow students to respond one at a time. After each reply, pull out one block from the stack and replace it on the top of the stack. You can even have students pull out the blocks as they reply to the question. Add a few responses of your own, as you continue to pull out blocks from the stack. Eventually the stack will fall over because of the faulty foundation. Discuss the following:

What are some of the shaky foundations we build our lives on?

What is it that makes a foundation firm or shaky?

What does it take to build a solid, firm foundation on Jesus Christ?

Make a transition into the study by talking about how our foundations are shaped by the standards and values by which we live.

IN THE WORD

Ask the following introductory questions:

How would you describe wisdom?

What is the difference between knowledge and wisdom?

Read James 3:13-18. Discuss the following:

1. How can you tell if a person is wise or not (see v. 13)?

2. How is worldly wisdom described in verses 14 and 15?

3. What is the natural outcome of worldly wisdom (see v. 16)?

4. How is godly wisdom described in verse 17?

5. What is the natural outcome of godly wisdom (see vv. 17,18)?

6. What happens when people "sow in peace"?

   What do you think that means?

7. How do we live by godly wisdom?

What Does It Take to Be Truly W-I-S-E?

I. **W = Wrestle with Worldliness**
   A. Examine your life and ask the question: Where am I buying into the world's standards and values?
   B. Make a decision to live your life by God's wisdom.
   C. Know that it's going to be a daily fight to live by God's wisdom.

II. **I = Investigate God's Word**
   A. Study God's Word for answers and for direction in life.
   B. Make God's Word your authority for your standards and values.
   C. God's Word is God's love letter to you. It is His truth and wisdom for each of us.
   D. We need to be in God's Word every day to be affected by it.

III. **S = Seek God in Prayer**
   A. Seek God in prayer about specific areas and directions in your life.
   B. Honestly bring your concerns and needs to Him—He cares about each of them.
   C. Pray specifically, often and honestly.
   D. Keep your eyes open to God's answers to prayer!

IV. **E = Enlist Others Who Are Godly**
  A. Seek out others that you see as godly, who live their lives by God's wisdom and standards.
  B. Ask advice of those people, seeking them out when you need direction.
  C. God can speak to us through others.
  D. You become like the people you hang out with.

Who do you want to be influenced by and be like?

So You Want to Be a Wise Guy!

1. Do you know anyone who fits the description of worldly wisdom? What is his or her life like?

   How does he or she fit the description?

2. Do you know anyone who fits the description of godly wisdom? What is his or her life like?

   How does he or she fit the description?

CHALLENGE/ACTION STEPS

What can you do this week to sow peace in a relationship?

Where do you need more godly wisdom this week?

What can you do this week to seek God's wisdom in that area?

Overview

Happily Ever After

TOPIC
Marriage and sex

DESCRIPTION
Getting married is perhaps one of the greatest moments in anyone's life. That's the way God planned it from the beginning. God created marriage and the promises that go along with it. He takes the biblical standard for marriage very seriously, and so should we when we promise our love to another person for a lifetime. This study takes a look at the institution of marriage and helps students understand the commitment required.

KEY VERSE
"'Haven't you read,' he replied, 'that at the beginning the Creator "made them male and female," and said, "For this reason a man will leave his father and mother and be united to his wife, and the two will become one flesh"? So they are no longer two, but one. Therefore, what God has joined together, let man not separate.'" Matthew 19:4-6

BIBLICAL BASIS
Genesis 1:28; 2:24,25; Matthew 19:4-6; Ephesians 5:22-33

THE BIG IDEA
God is the one who created the institution of marriage. He values it and takes our vows and promises within marriage seriously, just as we should.

AIMS OF THIS STUDY
In this study you will guide students to:
• Examine what God's Word says about marriage and sex;
• Discover the qualities of a godly marriage;
• Implement a lifestyle of abstinence, commitment to marriage and deciding to seek God's choice for their future spouses.

PREPARATION
For Challenge/Action Steps:
- 3x5-inch index cards, one for each student
- Pens or pencils

Outline

Happily Ever After

WARM-UP: SO WHAT DO YOU THINK?

Divide your meeting space down the middle. The far left side of the room will be the agree side and the far right side of the room will be the disagree side. Have the students stand. Instruct them to move to the appropriate side of the room based on whether they agree or disagree with the statements you will read. Following each statement, interact with a few students who agree and with a few who disagree.

1. Marriage was instituted by people.

2. Sex is bad and dirty.

3. The Bible has plenty to say about sex and marriage.

4. God thinks sex is sinful.

5. Sex is sacred and meant only for marriage.

6. The Bible talks about how men and women should act in marriage.

7. Marriage vows are just things you say to get married; they aren't really binding promises.

INTRODUCTION: WHAT DOES IT TAKE?

Read aloud Matthew 19:4-6 and discuss the following questions with the whole group:

1. What is marriage?

2. Who makes a commitment and to what do they commit?

3. What's involved in a marriage relationship?

4. What are marriage vows?

Read a typical set of marriage vows to the group. Have them define what's involved in each promise.

Divide the group into eight fairly even-sized small groups. Give each group one of the following eight vows. Allow each group 5 to 10 minutes to define what's involved in their assigned promise. Ask them to decide what the husband and wife are committing to and how that commitment might possibly be lived out.

Then have each group choose a representative to share with the others what they decided.

Option: You might give the students the option to act out their assigned vow with a skit. Either method works well.

1. To remain faithful

2. To stay committed during times of plenty and want

3. To stay committed in times of joy and sorrow

4. To stay committed during times of sickness and health

5. To forgive (love) one another

6. To strengthen (honor) one another

7. To join together to serve God and others

8. For as long as they both live

IN THE WORD
In the same small groups, have them work together to discover what God's plan for marriage is.

I. God's Plan for the Husband and Wife Relationship

Read Ephesians 5:22-33 and discuss the following questions.

1. What does God expect of a wife in a marital relationship?

2. What is she to do in relation to her husband?

3. What does "submit" or "be subject to" really mean?

4. What does God expect of a husband in a marital relationship?

5. What is he to do in relation to his wife?

6. What does "love your wife as Christ loved the church" really mean?

7. Does God require different things from the husband than from the wife? Why or why not?

8. How do the marital vows you discussed relate to these verses?

II. God's Plan for an Intimate Relationship

Make transition from the Ephesians passage to the Genesis passages by saying:

Because of the commitment we have made in marriage to bind us together as one flesh, we are able to share intimately everything about ourselves. We are free to be vulnerable and give those things which are most intimate to us to the one we love.

One of the most intimate things we can give is our sexuality. Because we have the assurance of life together forever with our spouses, there should be nothing holding us back from sharing ourselves with them. There is no risk when entering into a sexual relationship in marriage. It is truly the one and only form of safe sex. Read Genesis 1:28 and 2:24,25 to see God's perspective on sex.

Happily Ever After

In your small groups read Genesis 1:28 and Genesis 2:24,25, then discuss the following:

1. How does God view sex?

2. Who created sex?

3. What are two reasons it is important for married folks to have sex?

4. Why is it important to keep sex inside the confines of marriage?

5. God created sex to be beautiful. Why is sex sometimes viewed as ugly?

CHALLENGE/ACTION STEPS

You will be given an index card. Read the following instructions:

> Now that you better understand what is promised and what is expected in marriage, take some time to think about what you expect in your future spouse. Spend a few minutes writing out some specific characteristics, qualities and expectations you have for your future spouse. Be specific, be choosy and most of all, be biblical.
>
> Save this card to refer to in the future. You may want to revise it occasionally, but it would be interesting to see years down the road how close you came to marrying your perfect spouse and how your views of the "perfect" husband or wife have changed as you have been transformed to be more and more Christlike.

Close in prayer, praying for your future mate—that God would prepare and protect both of you for your future together. Make it a regular habit to pray for your future spouse and for your own preparation for marriage.

Overview

Getting the Ingredients Right

TOPIC
Ingredients for growing spiritually

DESCRIPTION
This study explores the essential ingredients for growing in our spiritual walk with Christ. Our desire is that students would be challenged to implement one or more of these ingredients if they are not already doing so.

KEY VERSE
"Being confident of this, that he who began a good work in you will carry it on to completion until the day of Christ Jesus." Philippians 1:6

BIBLICAL BASIS
Acts 2:42-47; Philippians 1:6; Colossians 3:17; Hebrews 10:24,25

THE BIG IDEA
Spiritual growth is the process of growing closer to God. God's Word gives us the ingredients to help in that process.

AIMS OF THIS STUDY
During this study you will guide students to:
- Examine how the first-century Church helped each other grow closer to God;
- Discover seven ingredients for spiritual growth;
- Implement one or more of the ingredients in their lives.

PREPARATION
For Introduction:
Before the meeting, buy the following items:
- Brown paper bag (ask that items be put into a paper bag at the store)

- Oreo cookies
- Bubble gum
- Twinkies
- Cleanser
- Spam
- I Can't Believe It's Not Butter! (butter substitute)
- Anything that has really strange ingredients

Before students arrive, place the items in the bag so no one can see them.

Outline

Getting the Ingredients Right

INTRODUCTION: WHAT ON EARTH IS IT?

To introduce the lesson ask students to guess what the items are by their ingredients. Then, holding the items inside the bag so they cannot be seen, read the ingredients of the items one at a time. After reading each list of ingredients, allow the group to try to guess what the item is. After using up the time or the items, explain:

> The ingredients are essential for each item. If you leave out one of the ingredients, the item will not be the same. So it is with our walk with Christ. There are ingredients for growing in your relationship with Christ that are essential. Without any one of these ingredients, you'd be missing out on the full experience of growth.

Discuss the following:

> What are some ingredients that will help you grow in your relationship with God?

> Which ingredients are the most important?

> Which could you really do without?

> What would your relationship be like without _____ being a part of it?
> *(list any ingredient)*

Explain:

> Today we'll be looking at some essential ingredients in the process of growing in our relationship with God.

IN THE WORD

In this section, you'll be looking at the ingredients for spiritual growth found in Acts 2:42-47. This is not an exhaustive list of growth ingredients, but it is a great passage on this issue. Feel free to add any ingredients not talked about in this lesson. Because of the amount of time you'll have, you won't be able to spend too much time on any one ingredient. Be sure to do the following:

- Define each ingredient.
- Explain its importance.
- Apply it to their lives.
- Talk about its impact on your own relationship with God.

Read Acts 2:42-47.

I. God's Word (v. 42)

    A. Spend personal time in God's Word.
    B. Listen to God's Word being taught.

II. Fellowship (v. 42)

    A. Develop relationships in small groups for accountability.
    B. Build relationships for the purpose of growth.

III. Prayer (v. 42)

    A. Adoration, Confession, Thanksgiving, Supplication (asking)—ACTS
    B. Listen for God's answers.

IV. Community (v. 44)

    A. Care for each other.
    B. Share our lives and material possessions.
    C. Encourage others.

V. Serving Others (v. 45)

    A. Serve people within the group, our church.
    B. Serve those outside the church.

VI. Worship (vv. 46,47)

- Give God His rightful place in our lives.

VII. Evangelize (v. 47)

    A. Share your faith with others.
    B. Love the lost.

Special Note:

The following discussion starters will help students personalize the ingredients for spiritual growth. The key will be in giving real-life examples of each ingredient and challenging students to apply one or two of the ingredients to their lives. Give students examples from your life. By opening up your life to them, they will feel more comfortable in talking about their own lives. Offer insight into where they are now in their spiritual growth processes and how they can get to where they want to be. Offer accountability to the group members in helping them live out one or more of the ingredients.

Getting the Ingredients Right

1. What is the difference between salvation and spiritual growth?

2. How does Philippians 1:6 relate to spiritual growth?

3. If someone is feeling spiritually dry and far away from God, what advice would you give him or her?

4. What has helped you grow the most in your relationship with God?

5. Who has been the greatest influence in your own spiritual growth?

   What has he or she done to encourage you to grow?

6. Which one or two of the ingredients is the toughest for you? Why?

7. If you could work on one spiritual ingredient in your life, which one would it be?

8. Read Hebrews 10:24,25. How can we help each other in growing closer to Christ?

CHALLENGE/ACTIONS STEPS

What will you do this coming week to work on this area?

Overview

Where Is God When It Hurts?

TOPIC
Pain and trials

DESCRIPTION
This study explores the issue of trials and testings. One of the most frequently asked questions by believers is, Where is God when I hurt? We all go through tough times—times of trials and testing. It's during those times that we ask tough questions. It's during those times that our faith is forged by the fire. Our hope is that through this study, students will be equipped to face those times with hope and faith.

KEY VERSE
"Consider it pure joy, my brothers, whenever you face trials of many kinds, because you know that the testing of your faith develops perseverance. Perseverance must finish its work so that you may be mature and complete, not lacking anything." James 1:2-4

BIBLICAL BASIS
Romans 5:1-5; James 1:1-18; 5:10,11; 1 Peter 1:3-9

THE BIG IDEA
Your circumstances may never change, but your attitude can, and that makes all the difference in the world.

AIMS OF THIS STUDY
During this study, you will guide students to:
* Examine the issue of trials in the life of the believer;
* Discover how God uses trials to bring maturity into the life of the believer;
* Implement an attitude of thankfulness, faith and trust toward trials in their personal lives.

PREPARATION

- A video of Olympic highlights
- A VCR and TV

Find a segment of the video that shows track or distance running events.

Outline

Where Is God When It Hurts?

INTRODUCTION: AN OLYMPIC-SIZED EFFORT

Show the video segment of track or distance running, then discuss the following questions:

What makes these athletes some of the greatest in the world?

What do you think it would take to win a gold medal at the Olympics?

What kind of training do you think they need to win?

Make the following observations to lead in to the subject of pain and trials in our lives:

- Athletes have to train to be able to win.
- To win, athletes have to push past the pain and the trials, focusing on the goals they have set for themselves.
- Athletes go through incredible training, pain, trials and sacrifices in order to attain the prize they so desperately compete for—to win, to be the best.

IN THE WORD

Explain:

All of us go through tough times and trials in our lives. No one is exempt! Our attitudes affect how we handle or react to tough times in our lives.

We can respond by:
- *Running Away*: trying to ignore them, going in the opposite direction
- *Running Around*: trying to hide from them, or trying to sidestep them altogether
- *Running Ahead*: taking them on, enduring them with the proper attitude

Discuss the following:

What is one trial that you have faced in the past month?

How did you react during that trial? (refer to the four *R*s)

Read James 1:1-18.

Let's look at some ways to respond with a positive attitude toward trials.

Three Keys to Having a Good Attitude, Not a Bad Attitude

I. **Key One: Choose to Have a Joyful Heart (see James 1:2-4)**
    A. Trials will come into your life. It's not a choice of *if*, but *when* they will come.
    B. We can rejoice because:
        1. Trials are opportunities for growth in faith and trust;
        2. We know we will be stronger after the trial for future battles (see v. 4);
        3. We know that God is at work in our lives. He uses our trials to strengthen and mature us.

Why does God allow people to go through trials and tough times?

How does a person's relationship with God change as he or she goes through trials and problems?

How can you choose to have a joyful heart?

What would you tell a friend who is going through a trial right now?

II. **Key Two: Come to God for Strength (see James 1:5-8)**
    A. God will strengthen you when you ask Him to.
    B. We need to ask continually for:
        1. Strength—to continue under the trial
        2. Wisdom—not to miss opportunities within the trials
        3. Perspective—to see trials through His eyes

What does verse 6 mean?

33

2242

What effect does doubt have on a person when he or she prays?

When do you find it hardest to pray?

With what doubts have you struggled concerning God and prayer?

How can a person seek God for strength? Wisdom? Perspective?

III. **Key Three: Chase After the Crown (see James 1:12)**
   A. The key to making it through trials is to look at the finish line, the goal, the prize.
   B. If we keep our eyes on the goal, we will make it through trials with style.
   C. Focus your eyes on Jesus Christ and what He's doing in your life through the trial.

What reward waits for the person who perseveres under trials?

What is the goal that we should be focused on?

What takes our focus off the goal during trials?

How can we regain our focus in the midst of trials?

Where Is God When It Hurts?

1. What do you think God is trying to teach you this week through the trials and situations you are facing?

2. In what areas do you need to ask God for His wisdom this week?

3. What temptations do you need God's help to resist this week?

CHALLENGE/ACTIONS STEPS

What can we do as a group to help one another keep focused on the goal?

Conclude in prayer for one another and for the trials group members are facing.

Scripture Reference Index

Old Testament

Bold numbers indicate Key Verses.

Bold numbers indicate Key Verses.

New Testament

Matthew

4:1-11	138
4:18-22	161
6:1-4	45
6:14,15	50, 199
6:24	95
6:25-32	193
6:25-34	125
6:34	**125**
7:1-6	187
9:35-38	33
9:37	176
9:37,38	**33**
11:29,30	76
12:34	66
12:34-37	27
14:14,18	155
14:22-33	131
14:31	**131**
18:21-35	199
19:4-6	**211**
20:26-28	95
23:12	95
28:16-20	176
28:19,20	**176**

Mark

10:43,44	**106**
10:43-45	106
12:30	**76**
12:31	**81**
14:31,50	71

Luke

1:26-38	161
4:13	138
10:30-37	81
12:27-30	155
15:11-24	50
15:20	**50**
17:11-19	61
23:32-34	199

John

1:12	**89**
3:1-21	89
3:16	50
6:1-15	155
6:9	**155**

Bold numbers indicate Key Verses.

6:38	161	5:1-5	223
8:1-11	17, 113	5:3-5	**171**
8:2-11	50	5:8	61, 76
8:31,32	55	8:12-17,38,39	89
13:1-17	106	8:15	144
13:34,35	81	8:15,16,35-39	100
15:10,11	55	8:28	171
16:33	55	8:31,32,37-39	193
17:17	55	8:38,39	50
20:19-31	181	12:1,2	66, 95
		13:8	81

Acts

1:8	176	15:4	150
2:42-47	217		

1 Corinthians

9:1-19	161	6:18-20	113
9:26,27	27	9:24,25	119
10	166	10:13	**113**, 138
11:1-19	166	12:12,13	81
11:18	**166**	13:4-7	113

2 Corinthians

11:22,23	27	5:17	81
15:1-29	166	5:17-20	33
15:37-40	27	9:6-8	45

Romans

Galatians

4:7	50	5:16	113
4:18-21	38		

Bold numbers indicate Key Verses.

Bold numbers indicate Key Verses.

Bold numbers indicate Key Verses.

More Great Ways to Reach and Teach Young People

So You Want to Be a Wise Guy
An outrageous group study for junior high
Manual
ISBN 08307.29178

Dave's Complete Guide to Junior High Ministry
An all-in-one, practical, hands-on guide for everything relating to junior high ministry
Dave Veerman
Paperback
ISBN 08307.27604

GP4U (God's Plan for You)
A middle school/junior high group study
Kara Eckmann Powell
Reproducible
ISBN 08307.24060

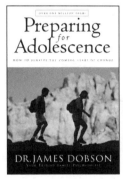

Preparing for Adolescence
Dr. James Dobson
Paperback
ISBN 08307.24974

Guide to Childhood Development
Mass
ISBN 08307.24990

Family Guide and Workbook
Manual
ISBN 08307.25016

Growth Guide Manual
ISBN 08307.25024

Group Guide
ISBN 08307.25008

Family Tape Pack—8 Audiocassettes
ISBN 08307.26357

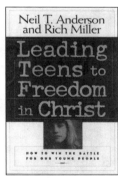

Leading Teens to Freedom in Christ
How to win the battle for our young people
Neil T. Anderson
and *Rich Miller*
Paperback
ISBN 08307.18400

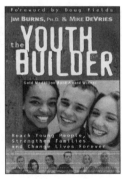

The YouthBuilder
Reaching young people for Christ and changing lives forever
Jim Burns
and *Mike DeVries*
Paperback
ISBN 08307.29232

Gospel Light

Available at your local Christian bookstore
www.gospellight.com

Wake 'Em Up!

This fresh-roasted blend of sizzling hot resources helps you turn youth meetings into dynamic events that kids look forward to. Successfully field-tested in youth groups and edited by youth expert **Jim Burns, Fresh Ideas** will wake 'em up and get your group talking.

Bible Study Outlines and Messages
ISBN 08307.18850

Case Studies, Talk Sheets and Starters
ISBN 08307.18842

Games, Crowdbreakers & Community Builders
ISBN 08307.18818

Illustrations, Stories and Quotes to Hang Your Message On
ISBN 08307.18834

Incredible Retreats
ISBN 08307.24036

Missions and Service Projects
ISBN 08307.18796

Skits and Dramas
ISBN 08307.18826

Worship Experiences
ISBN 08307.24044

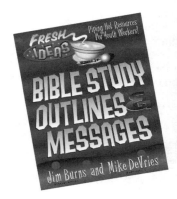
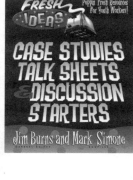

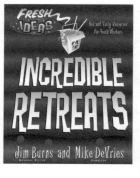

Gospel Light

To wake up your youth, contact your local Christian bookstore. **www.gospellight.com**

Pulse

GOD'S WORD FOR A JR. HIGH WORLD

Young people between the ages of 11 and 14 are the most open to who Jesus is and what a life with Him offers. Reach them with Pulse—designed especially for them!

Throughout the cutting-edge series, three categories of study help junior highers understand and apply God's Word in their lives: Biblical, Life Issues and Discipleship.

Connect with junior highers—get all the Pulse studies!

#1 Christianity: the Basics
ISBN 08307.24079

#2 Prayer
ISBN 08307.24087

#3 Friends
ISBN 08307.24192

#4 Teachings of Jesus
ISBN 08307.24095

#5 Followers of Christ
ISBN 08307.24117

#6 Teens of the Bible
ISBN 08307. 24125

#7 Life at School
ISBN 08307.25083

#8 Miracles of Jesus
ISBN 08307.25091

#9 Home and Family
ISBN 08307.25105

#10 Genesis
ISBN 08307.25113

#11 Fruit of the Spirit
ISBN 08307.25474

#12 Feelings & Emotions
ISBN 08307.25482

#13 Peer Pressure
ISBN 08307.25490

#14 Reaching Your World
ISBN 08307.25504

Available at your local Christian bookstore.
www.gospellight.com

Gospel Light

041633

More from Jim Burns, the Youth Ministry Expert!

Why I Sponsor A Child Through Compassion

As a youth worker, I'm always looking for practical ways to challenge the kids and families I get to be around. Recently, the WWJD (What Would Jesus Do?) Campaign has been immensely popular—almost trendy. Rather than trying to speculate, "what would Jesus do," maybe we should simply respond to the question "what DID He do?" No question but that one of His highest priorities was that of responding to the needs of the "least of these." And, He's challenged us to do the same.

I can't think of anything more important in life than helping impact the world in which we live by meeting the needs of hurting children. Many child sponsorship organizations exist to help people do just that!

Compassion International does it best!

I've had the privilege of visiting some of Compassion's projects in Ecuador. I came away impressed that each project is run exclusively by Christians who are committed to helping each child get the best possible start in life—and an opportunity to receive new life in Jesus Christ.

Just 80 cents a day ($24 a month) provides desperately needy kids access to educational opportunities, health screening, and supplemental food. Great return for a minimal investment. *Smart Money*, a magazine of the *Wall Street Journal*, included Compassion (the only child sponsorship organization) in a list of ten charities they said give the "most bang for your buck!"

But, it's not just about money and good stewardship. This is what I really like about Compassion. Sponsors get to be personally involved by building a relationship with their sponsored child. As a sponsor, you'll receive your child's photo and personal story. You can exchange letters and even send an additional amount for gifts on birthdays or at Christmas. Our entire family looks forward to receiving letters from our sponsored children, Ramiro Moises Santi and Ruth Irlanda Cando Cuenca, and hopes to actually visit them someday. The child you sponsor will know you by name and appreciate your love, help, and prayers.

Won't you join with me in giving a needy child a new start today by completing this coupon or by calling Compassion's toll-free number?

Jim Burnes and his family sponsor Ramiro Moises Santi and Ruth Irlanda Cando Cuenca.

Yes! I want to give a life-changing gift to one child in need.

Please select a child who needs my love and prayers. Send me his or her photo, personal story, and a complete sponsorship packet. If I decide to become a sponsor, I'll send my first monthly sponsorship check for $24 at that time.

My preference is: ❏ a boy ❏ a girl ❏ either
From: ❏ Africa ❏ Asia ❏ South America
❏ Central America ❏ any location

❏ I want to begin immediately.

My first sponsorship support is enclosed as follows: ❏ $24 (one month) ❏ $72 (three months)

Name _____

Address _____

City _____

State _____ Zip _____

Telephone (____) _____

Sponsorship is tax-deductible and receipts will be sent.

QUESTIONS? CALL (800) 336-7676
or visit our Web site at www.compassion.com

COMPASSION™
INTERNATIONAL
Colorado Springs, Colorado 80997

ECFA

335975004